GHOSTS IN CORNWALL

'When you have eliminated the impossible, whatever remains, however improbable, must be the truth.'

Sherlock Holmes, 'The Sign of Four.'

MARGARET BLAGGE from the portrait by Mary Beale at Stonor Park.

Photo by courtesy of Macmillan & Co. (*Chapter 8*)

GHOSTS IN CORNWALL

A New Look at Hauntings in the South West

Eric Hirth

First Edition published June 1986.

© Eric Hirth

Printed & Published by:
The St. Ives Printing & Publishing Company,
High Street, St. Ives, Cornwall. Tel. (0736) 795813.

ISBN 0 948385 04 9.

CONTENTS

ACKNOWLEDGEMENTS

I am extremely grateful for the generous help and willing co-operation which I have received from all the people whose experiences with paranormal forces are described in these stories. My own task has been simply to record the facts, but the stories are theirs. I hope I have done them justice.

For drawing my attention to some interesting cases which I would certainly otherwise have missed, I am indebted to miss Barbara Blackwell, Mr. Brian Crick, Mr. Michael Hughes, Mrs. Sue Legge, Mr. John Rogers, Mrs. Joan Sheldrake, Mr. Mark Thomas and Mr. and Mrs. Brian Trevorrow.

Special thanks are due to my wife, who accompanied me on these and many other excursions into the twilight world of ghosts. Her gift of total recall enabled her not only to correct errors in my notes but also to add several important details which I had overlooked.

Eric Hirth,
St. Ives, Cornwall.   February 1986.

INTRODUCTION

CERTAIN areas of England seem to attract a greater incidence of paranormal activity than others. Every county of course has its ghost-lore and its crop of haunted places, but the evidence suggests that Cornwall enjoys the dubious distinction of being the most ghost-ridden county of them all.

To track down, investigate and report on even half the alleged hauntings in the Duchy would be a formidable if not impossible task, and for this reason I have chosen to present the reader with a selection of the more interesting cases which have come to my notice within a limited area of some twenty miles around St. Ives, in which town, incidentally, the concentration of psychic activity is particularly high.

Unfortunately it is the sad lot of every psychical investigator to be plagued at every turn by baseless rumours, inaccurate and misleading reports and all manner of wildly improbable stories, all of which nevertheless have to be looked into and evaluated for what they might be worth. At best, sightings of supernatural beings are always difficult to substantiate, even from the most obviously genuine sources, and one may have to wait a long time to establish whether a reported 'sighting' is a one-off event or whether the ghost has been seen by other people over a period of time. This could be of cardinal importance in deciding what is a haunting and what is not.

In the chapters ahead I have avoided legends and tales of unknown origin, all the incidents and stories here having been garnered entirely from conversations which I have been privileged to enjoy with the people most closely involved, whose complete honesty and sincerity I have no reason to doubt. It would be presumptious to insist that every incident described is of supernatural origin, and indeed I have once or twice suggested alternative possibilities, but a great deal still remains which is inexplicable in rational terms.

Obviously, the credibility of any ghost story depends upon whether we accept that the human personality survives physical death, since without this fundamental belief there is no case for the existence of ghosts except as some kind of mental aberration on the part of those who claim to see them. Bernard Shaw remarked that belief is not dependant on evidence and reason, but is literally a matter of taste. For instance, a great many people accept the Arthurian legend as historical fact despite the lack of any reliable evidence that King Arthur even existed. If challenged, such people would doubtless tell you that until it has been proved that Arthur did *not* exist they will continue to assume that he did. By the same token one might answer those who insist that no evidence has ever been produced to prove that there is life after death by pointing out that neither has any evidence been produced to prove that there is not.

To the lay mind, the word 'haunting' is synonymous with the appearance of some sort of apparition, but in fact it includes a widely differing assortment of phenomena in which the actual sighting of a ghost plays little or no part at all, as in the case of that most baffling of domestic hauntings known as Poltergeist, characterized by bangings, rappings and the throwing around of household objects, including items of furniture, often with great violence. This kind of psychic disturbance is somewhat in a class of its own with a behaviour pattern alien to most other hauntings in that it tends to start suddenly and then cease altogether, sometimes in a matter of weeks. Investigators have noted that it seems to occur mostly in houses which include an adolescent among the occupants, the theory being that the entity draws its power and its ability to activate from some kind of psychic 'leak' emanating from the young, and whilst there is a great deal of evidence to suggest that this almost certainly is the case, the fact remains that Poltergeist disturbances frequently manifest where no adolescents are present, also in places other than family dwellings.

But ghosts do not need to be either seen or heard for their presence to be known. An acquaintance of mine says that he always knows when his late father's spirit is around when he smells the fragrance of a well-known brand of tobacco much favoured by the deceased gentleman during his earthly life, and indeed many investigators have remarked upon the smells of perfume which come and go in haunted places. A howl of derision greeted Sir Arthur Conan Doyle's assertion that his dead son Raymond appeared smoking a cigar and with a glass of whiskey in his hand, but it seems not unreasonable to believe that we do not abandon earthly pleasures in the next life, at least until we find we have no further need of them!

Regarding apparations, I share the view held by most researchers that only a small percentage of reported sightings are genuine spirit manifestations, although that is not to say that all the rest are either imagined or invented. It frequently happens that a psychically gifted person entering an old building will pick up impressions from the many layers of its history, and perhaps even describe the physical appearance of a long-dead owner, but this kind of subjective experience, interesting and informative though it may be, is no indication of a ghost presence.

How does one define a ghost? Professor Hans Holzer, the noted Austrian-born parapsychologist, has this to say:

'Apparitions of "dead" people, or sounds associated with invisible human beings, are the surviving emotional memories of people who have not been able to make the transition from the physical state into the world of spirit. Such people are totally unable to adjust or recognize or accept the change to another type of existence and become so-called ghosts. Really they are parts of a human personality left in the physical world but no longer able to function in it.'*

This is a brilliant analysis, and I shall not attempt to add to it except to remark that whatever it is that keeps these unfortunates earth-bound, be it the pursuit of some unfinished business or because, as Holzer suggests, some people cannot accept death, or indeed may not even know they *are* dead, their presence should evoke not feat but pity.

I am told by those who have seen ghosts that, aside from a habit of abruptly vanishing or walking through walls and closed doors, they seem to be as solid and real as the rest of us, which disposes once and for all of the transparent spook image beloved by cartoonists and illustrators of fictional horror stories. It also suggests that we may see ghosts more frequently than we suppose.

Perhaps we should look more closely at that quiet man sitting opposite in the railway carriage, or that woman in black standing on the street corner. They may not be as solid or real as they seem!

*'The Ghost Hunters.' Peter Underwood, 1985.

Chapter One

'THE OLD ONES'

THE 'Halfway House' at Fraddam was serving drinks as early as the fourteenth-century. Originally a thatched farmhouse offering rest and refreshment to pilgrims on their way to the monastery at St. Michael's Mount, it was rebuilt in the seventeenth-century and has a granite fireplace which is undoubtedly one of the finest examples of its kind in the county. One evening during the nineteen-sixties Mrs. 'Frankie' Holman and her husband Paul were enjoying a quiet drink at this historic Inn.

'Suddenly,' Mrs. Holman told me, 'one side of me went freezing cold and I felt that someone was staring at me. I looked in the direction from which these sensations seemed to be coming and I saw, sitting in a corner seat which had up till then been empty, the outline of a rather plump lady wearing a poke-bonnet and a full skirt. I couldn't see her face yet I knew she was staring at me. Paul, who noticed the expression on my face, said "Whatever's the matter?" I said "can you see anybody in that corner?" He said no, he couldn't, and when I looked again the figure was gone. The strange thing is that for the rest of the evening, despite the fact that only a few locals were in, I could hear Cornishmens' voices filling the whole pub, as though both bars were crammed with miners or market-gardeners come in for a drink after their day's labours.'

Taken in isolation, the hubbub of voices might be explained in a number of ways, the most obvious being that Mrs. Holman was suffering from mental fatigue resulting in some kind of aural distortion, not at all an uncommon thing in cases of extreme tiredness, but the figure in the corner contains all the classic elements of a genuine ghost manifestation, so the whole story needs to be looked at more closely.

First, however, let us see what Mrs. P. Brett has to tell us about her own encounter with supernatural forces at a time when she was living at Mousehole, the ancient fishing village which earned a place in Cornish History back in 1595, when the crews of four Spanish galleons which had become separated from the disintegrating Armada landed there and burnt the place down, probably out of sheer frustration.

During the winter of 1976 Mrs. Brett's dog had been ill, and very early one morning presented himself at his mistress's bedside with an urgent request to be let out. It was still only four o'clock, but the valiant Mrs. Brett, unwilling to allow her pet out on his own at such an hour, threw on some clothes and led the animal into the grey, silent streets towards the beach. The dog however, held back, refusing to make the short journey down to the beach and showing unfamiliar signs of fear.

'All of a sudden,' Mrs. Brett told me, 'I heard footsteps. I thought, who is about at this time? Then it seemed to be a lot of footsteps, as if dozens of people were scurrying about with purpose. No voices, but this busy sound of people going about their business as though perhaps fishermen were preparing to go to sea.'

Convinced that she was in the middle of some supernatural phenomenon, and by now thoroughly alarmed, Mrs. Brett retreated back into her home before realising that her unfortunate dog had yet to relieve himself. Summoning up her courage she went again into the street hoping the ghostly footsteps had ceased, instead of which she heard them agian, this time from another direction. 'I was terrified,' she said. 'Nothing would induce me to go into the village and past the "Ship."'[1] At no time during this episode did Mrs. Brett see anyone on the streets, nor did she hear the sound of a human voice.

Inevitably, one looks for a rational explanation to account for this strange happening. Did Mrs. Brett, called from her bed at that most uncongenial of hours, hallucinate? But in that case why was her dog so alarmed?

The ghostly re-enactment of past events is by no means an uncommon phenomenon, more particularly events associated with violence, or some other strong emotion. One of the most famous cases of this kind was at Edge Hill, on the Warwicks and Northants borders where, as every schoolboy knows, a fierce and bloody battle took place during the civil war in 1642. A few months after the battle, terrified peasants in the neighbourhood reported seeing phantom armies approaching one another at this spot, and hearing the clash of arms, the screams and groans of the wounded and so on. King Charles himself ultimately heard of these extraordinary rumours and sent a group of his officers to investigate. It seems that they too witnessed the phantom battle. In recent years sporadic reports from the area suggest that, although images and sounds still occur, they are becoming weaker and less frequent. Perhaps after three hundred years this perplexing manifestation is fading.

Visitors to Hampton Court palace are told the equally well-known story of the ghost of Catherine Howard, seen at times running towards the Chapel seeking sanctuary, presumably from the wrath of King Henry after Cranmer had uncovered her extra-marital activities. But supernatural occurences such as these raise many questions. It is as difficult to credit that the unquiet spirit of poor Catherine is still running around after four hundred years as it is to believe that thousands of earth-bound warriors find themselves re-enacting a particularly horrendous battle for which many of them doubtless had little enough enthusiasm in the first place. What then is the explanation?

One interesting theory suggests that such incidents are recorded on the ether[2] rather in the manner of a movie camera recording on film, so that

[1] Mousehole's only Inn, facing the Harbour.

[2] In modern physics, an elastic and subtle substance believed to permeate all space. The medium through which waves of light are propagated.—(Oxford English Dictionary).

what is being witnessed is, to use a contemporary analogy, an 'action replay' of the original event. In other words we are seeing, or hearing, or both, recorded impressions not ghosts.

Mrs. Holman and Mrs. Brett may well have experienced time-slips and strayed into pockets of 'recorded' history, even though neither of them can tell us what the commotions they heard were all about. But not every detail fits snugly into this analysis. I still wonder what frightened Mrs. Brett's dog?

Perhaps, after all, ghosts were abroad in the chilly Mousehole dawn, for the locals will tell you they have plenty of them in their village. Like all the Cornish, they affect a delightful nonchalance towards this embarrassment of spectral riches in their midst, and when they speak of them — which isn't often — they call them simply 'The Old Ones,' a term handed down through the centuries, and as old as the village itself.

Chapter Two

THE LONE HORSEMAN

ASK any Cornishman living in this part of the county if he knows where Kerris is, and he will quite likely have to think long and hard before he can tell you, yet this strangely obscure farmland area is less than four miles from busy Newlyn. History is to be found there in the shape of an ancient manor-house, part mediaeval and part Tudor, but now a sad ruin except for the front portion, which was restored early in the eighteenth century and is currently occupied.

Late one evening in the autumn of 1948, Mr. Bill Picard, whose home is on the outskirts of Kerris, was walking near the manor-house when he was surprised to see a figure on horseback ambling across the path in front of him. There had been heavy rain, and since at that time the roads round there were unmade and little more than muddy tracks, Mr. Picard was more concerned with avoiding puddles than in observing the horse and its rider, which vanished in the direction of some farm cottages. But he did have time to notice that the man was wearing what appeared to be a military greatcoat and a small round hat which looked to be made of fur.

At that period, just three years after the end of the second world war, it was not unusual to see farm labourers and other manual workers wearing army or air force overcoats salvaged from their Service days or obtained from Government surplus stores, so that Mr. Picard assumed the man to be a farm worker returning home from one of the many farms in the area, and gave the matter no further thought.

Twenty years after this seemingly trifling incident, that is in 1968, Mr. Picard chanced to be walking along the same road, which by now had been tar macadamed, and again it was an autumn night, this time fine with a bright moon shining. At precisely the same spot where he had seen the horse and its rider he was astonished to see them again crossing his path, but this time he had the added impression that the horse was being led by someone other than the rider, who sat motionless with both his hands in front of him. Mr. Picard was able to look more closely at the rider's greatcoat, which he described as being drawn in at the waist after the fashion of coats worn by army officers during the early part of the nineteenth century. It was only later he recalled the startling fact that the horse's hooves had made no sound on the now hardened surface of the road.

The sighting of this unusual apparition for the second time in twenty years, in the same place and before the same witness, does not of course preclude the liklihood of it having appeared during the intervening years as well, if anyone happened to be around to see it. However, since that time it has made at least one sensational visit, as we shall see.

A year or two following Mr. Picard's second encounter with the ghost, some friends of his, Mr. and Mrs. W. L. Tudor of Penzance were enjoying a holiday in their former home town of Wrexham in North Wales. Visiting old friends there one day they learnt that their hosts' daughter Rosemary, together with her husband and young child, had been on a camping holiday in Cornwall.

It had been a disaster.

Pressed by Mr. Tudor for further details he was asked if he knew a place called Kerris, for it was here in a field that Rosemary and her family had pitched their tent. On their first night they were disturbed by the sound of horses' hooves clumping around the field, but when morning came there was no sign of any horses, which puzzled but did not especially worry them. On the second night however, Rosemary awoke in terror to see a man on horseback ride straight through the tent, and promptly flung herself across the body of her sleeping child, convinced that they were about to be trampled to death. The coming of daylight showed no damage or sign of physical entry into the tent, and the field was as deserted as it had been since their arrival. The unhappy campers, by this time thoroughly unnerved, hastily packed their belongings and left for home.

Mr. Tudor listened to this story in amazement. He already knew from his friend Mr. Picard about the phantom horseman, and here was corroborative evidence being supplied in a chance conversation with people who could have had no pre-knowledge of the haunting.

As to the identity of the horseman, the possibilities are endless. Being an 'outdoor' ghost, so to speak, there is no obvious point of origin to begin an investigation, although the manor-house seems as likely as anywhere to provide a clue. Indeed, near the entrance to the restored portion there stands a fine specimen of a stepped horse-mounting block. The indications are that it is not *in situ,* but it has nevertheless been in its present position for very many years, and may well have been used by the ghost rider during his lifetime.

A locally based historian, Mrs. Elizabeth Sparrow, who has made a special study of the area around Kerris, told me that in the course of its long history the manor-house frequently had as many as three owners at one and the same time, sole ownership of the huge house having bankrupted quite a few distinguished families. Early in the nineteenth-century a certain Lt. Col. Oxnam of the Mounts Bay regiment (an amalgam of various Penzance and district corps, later to be known as the Local Militia) was in possession of the house, and he may well be the marauding horseman, particularly having regard to Mr. Picards's description of the uniform.

But there is another aspect of this intriguing case which came to light during my talk with Mrs. Sparrow. It seems the road from the coast through Kerris was in constant use by smugglers, and we know that the militia was used to help the Revenue men round up these 'honest thieves' as Charles Lamb called them. Could it be that the sound of horses' hooves heard by the campers and the seeming intrusion of a rider into their tent was a psychic 'replay' of one of these violent and often bloody encounters between soldiery and smugglers?

This is an area which seems to offer an interesting variety of paranormal phenomena. Mousehole has already been mentioned in the previous chapter, and there is a well-known haunted place at Lamorna. Surprisingly, the ghosts of hooded monks have several times been sighted on the roads between St. Buryan and Paul, though I suspect that these may not be ghosts as such, but rather the 'thought vibrations' left by these holy men in the course of their constant perambulations throughout the county in the long distant past, when a Benedictine monastery flourished on the Island rock of St. Michael.

LUCY JENKINS' cottage in St. John's-street, Hayle.

(Chapter 13).

THE intersection of two lanes at Kerris, where the horseman was twice seen.
(Chapter 2)

'CURLEWS' during the nineteen-fifties, when still a private residence.

Photo by courtesy of Mrs. A. Guthrie. *(Chapter 5)*

THE gate leading to Foage Farm. It marks the precise spot where the injured cyclist was observed.

(Chapter 6)

THE centre window of the "King's Room" at Godolphin.

(Chapter 8)

Chapter Three

THE SAD FATE OF MRS. BAINES

THE notorious and much chronicled Borley Rectory on the Essex-Suffolk borders came to be dubbed "The Most Haunted House in England," and the village of Pluckley in Kent, with its dozen or so ghosts, is often called "The Most Haunted Village." Graceful and historic Chapel-street in Penzance might well qualify for the title of the most haunted street, for it is quite literally full of ghosts.

Number Eighteen was, if its history has been correctly recorded, a mansion owned in the early nineteenth-century by a Mrs. Baines, who was accidentally shot and killed by her manservant in the orchard at the rear of the building. Her ghost has reputedly haunted the place ever since. Number Eighteen is now the "Peninsula Restaurant," a family business owned and managed by Mr. and Mrs. Peter Walker together with their son and daughter-in-law Nicholas and Muriel, and it was in the latters' sitting-room above the restaurant that Mr. Walker junior talked to me about the strange happenings which suggest that Mrs. Baines is still around after a century and a half.

'We hear heavy footsteps in the loft above this room,' he told me. 'It is never used and we don't go up there if we can help it, but I understand it was a bedroom many years ago. The footsteps are heard most often between nine and ten o'clock in the evening, but we are generally busy in the restaurant at that time, so we aren't often bothered by the sounds.' On one memorable occasion, after the vicar from the church next door had called to make arrangements for the christening of their younger child the ghost 'went berserk' and kept the Walkers up half the night banging and crashing around.

Mr. Walker has an intriguing theory to account for this. It seems that at one time a local parson was called in to exorcise the ghost. For a time the ceremony appears to have been successful, but the haunting started up again and Mr. Walker thinks that the presence of another cleric scared it into assuming another exorcism was being planned!

Muriel Walker then took up the story. 'One morning I awoke early hearing my little girl crying, and got up to attend to her. Suddenly there was a loud, frantic knocking on what sounded like the kitchen door, and our dog began barking furiously. Thinking someone had come into the flat — my father-in-law does have a key — I ran to see who was knocking, and why, but all the doors were locked and there was nobody about. I felt very scared.'

Apparently the ghost does not confine its activities to the Walkers' flat. The occupants of other flats within this large and complex building have experienced the footsteps and there are at least two reports of actual sightings, although I have not been able to confirm these claims, which have not, by the way, been made by any of the Walker family.

But there was, for a time, a far more worrying feature of this haunting. Soon after they had moved into the flat various articles, some trivial, some quite valuable, simply disappeared. The Walkers gave me two examples out of many.

There was the time when Muriel removed her wrist-watch in order to wash her hands or perform some domestic detail or other, and when she turned to retrieve it, the watch had vanished. They carried out a thorough search, even removing some of the floor boards, but to no avail. It has not been seen since. On another occasion a costly pair of hand-made shoes belonging to a man friend staying at the flat disappeared from his room. 'Burglary was out of the question,' Mr. Walker remarked. 'We owned an eleven-stone bull mastiff at the time. No burglar would have got past him. Besides, the flat was undisturbed and there were no signs of a break-in.' The shoes, a hefty pair of number elevens, seemed to have melted, literally, into thin air.

The dematerialization of solid objects is perhaps the least credible of all supernatural phenomena. Our natural scepticism forces us to reject such a notion, yet many instances of it have been recorded from time to time in the history of psychical research. Usually the articles are returned in some 'jokey' fashion such as dropping from the ceiling in front of the owners, but there is evidence that sometimes the missing articles turn up hundreds and even thousands of miles away from their original provenance.

What purpose this puckish behaviour serves, if any, I do not know, but it does at least raise one important issue: how can solid objects be manipulated in this extraordinary manner by spirit forces? Surely this calls into question our whole concept of the nature of matter? Regrettably it is beyond the scope and intent of this book to attempt a dissertation on such esoteric subjects, and in the meantime it will provide Mrs. Walker with little comfort to be told that her watch may have materialized at a Hampstead séance or that it has fallen into the lap of a praying monk in Tibet. Perhaps after all she may one day walk into her flat and find that the watch has been returned, in which case let us hope the spirit pranksters have at least had the courtesy to keep it wound up!

But is the late Mrs. Baines really responsible for all these happenings? I am not at all sure. The footsteps, the bangings, the pilferings, the occasional pandemonium, all these things are symptomatic of a Poltergeist haunting, which would infer that the entity causing these disturbances is not necessarily connected with the Baines affair. There are, of course, the reported sightings, so we cannot rule out the possibility that Mrs. Baines is around. Mr. Walker tells me that nothing has vanished from the flat for a long time, and suggests that the ghost has 'come to live in harmony with us.' It maybe so, but it is worth remembering that Poltergeist activity almost always ceases after a while.

Finally let us not forget the unfortunate manservant who fired the shot which killed Mrs. Baines, and whose anguish must have been acute. Could it be *his* heavy footsteps which are heard above the Walkers' sitting-room? Surely, as a servant, he is more likely to have occupied an attic bedroom than his mistress?

THE section of Lethlean-lane referred to in Chapter 9. The figure in the photograph is standing by the old farm gate.

'THE OLD INN' at Mullion Village.

(Chapter 14)

Chapter Four

A ROYAL HIDE-OUT

ON high ground to the north of Penzance stands one of the most private, and consequently least known, of all the historic houses in the South West: Treneere Manor.

Once surrounded by its own vast acres of farmland, a sprawling housing estate now reaches almost to its back door, but happily the high walls and exotic trees and shrubs which abound in Treneere's extensive gardens help to preserve the illusion that the world outside looks much the same as it did in 1758, when the present house was built.

Mr. G. R. Symons, whose ancestral home it is, told me that his more distant forebears also owned an Elizabethan mansion which formerly stood on the site, and in fact the Symons' have been there in an unbroken sequence since the middle of the fourteenth-century. In the courtyard at the rear of the house a small section of the Tudor building still remains and is being painstakingly restored at this moment, and close by are the ruins of what was once a row of cells, the precise purpose of which has to be a matter for conjecture.

Pack-horses carrying tin and copper from the mines used to come here for the metals to be stamped before being taken to Mousehole for shipping, and were frequently waylaid by marauding bands of robbers. Mr. Symons thinks that the cells may have been built to accommodate those who were caught until they could be handed over to the Justices, but the fact that instruments of torture were discovered among the ruins suggests that the cells were there for more covert reasons than the mere incarceration of felons.

The present house is a typical Georgian rectangle, sturdily built of granite blocks, and is a fine example of its kind. In its spacious and beautiful dining-hall my wife and I sat before a huge log-fire while Mr. Symons told us something of the manor's remarkable history and of his own experiences with a supernatural being whose identity has not been established.

He first became aware of a ghost in the house when, as a young lad, he awoke one night to hear heavy footsteps 'like someone with hobnailed boots' descending the front staircase. At the time, the only occupants besides himself were two elderly aunts whose bedroom was on the same level as his own, and a housekeeper and servant who slept at the top of the house. Unlikely though it seemed that his aunts would have been clumping around the house in hobnailed boots, or for that matter any other footwear, in the middle of the night, he nevertheless felt moved to ask them the next morning if they had left their room.

'Certainly not,' they said, 'you must have heard *Him*.'

'And who is *Him?*' their nephew asked.

'We don't know,' they told him. 'We have heard those steps ever since we have been here.'

The aunts had lived there from around 1875 and had obviously accepted the presence of a ghost as something one learned to live with, and, after a while, ignore altogether. But young Symons was far from satisfied with this ambiguous answer. Suspecting that a marauder was hiding somewhere in the building he sat that night with a double-barrelled shot gun across his knees until he heard the footsteps, then began a meticulous search through the rooms and corridors without encountering either man or spirit. In the end he had to accept that the footsteps were probably of supernatural origin and in the course of time lost interest, or just slept through them.

An interesting sidelight on these ghostly perambulations is that they sometimes occur when the family is up and about. They hear the footsteps descend the stairway and cross the hall, followed by the sound of a door opening and closing. As a matter of course they always investigate, but there is never anybody to be seen. Their pet Labrador dog would on no account venture near the staircase, but their bull-terrier 'Keeper' used to stand at the foot of it looking up and barking furiously, his hackles raised, which suggests that he saw what everybody else merely heard!

In 1966 events took a strange turn. Mr. Symons had suffered a severe illness — a legacy from his war service days — and in order to avoid undue stair-climbing he abandoned his bedroom high in the building, and on his doctor's advice moved to another one on the first floor. But there was no bathroom on that level, and a problem arose as to how and where to put one. The only adjacent rooms were the breakfast room and the library, and it was unthinkable that they should be interfered with. However, there seemed to be a considerable area of space under the stairs, concealed by wood panelling. Could a bathroom be built there?

After consultation with his carpenter a cautious hole was bored into the woodwork with brace and bit, which to their surprise when withdrawn bore traces of brick dust. On Mr. Symons' instructions the panelling was removed to disclose a thin brick wall, which they quickly demolished, and this in turn revealed a little secret room furnished with a seat, a lead wash-basin and a lead toilet together with a soil pipe, which ran through the wall from above, indicating that there must be another similar room higher up in the building, although they have made no attempt to locate it.

Later they found a trap-door let into the staircase by which the lower room was entered, but how did the occupier breathe fresh air? Then Mr. Symons recalled that he had noticed a gap between two of the granite blocks high up on the outside wall, which he had intended to have repointed then forgot about. He checked its position and found the gap to be on the same level as the secret room — obviously an air vent.

He told me that he had always been aware that the present and former mansions were known as 'safe houses' intended to hide persons of high birth fleeing from religious or political persecution, and he has good reason for believeing that one auspicious fugitive who stayed at the former house was King Charles the Second. It is well known that Charles travelled to the South-West and thence to the Scilly Isles after his disastrous clash with Cromwell's forces at Worcester, and secluded Treneere was probably the only mansion not known to Cromwell's spies, besides being the nearest 'safe house' to the harbour of Mousehole, where a ship would have taken him across to the Isles.

The little room was cleared, work then commencing on the laying of a new floor, and it was at this point that a new and startling incident took place.

Late one afternoon, Mr. Symons was talking with some friends in a room below when a violent banging started up 'like someone using a sledge-hammer,' apparently from the floor above. He turned to his housekeeper and asked if Mr. Eddy (the carpenter) was still working, as it seemed rather late for him to be there. 'No,' she said, 'he left an hour ago.' They went upstairs to investigate and found the carpenter's tools, which he always stacked away before leaving, strewn all around the floor. They left them where they were and checked with the astonished carpenter next day, who assured Mr. Symons that he had put all the tools in his bag before leaving.

But this was not the first instance of Poltergeist activity at Treneere. In the nearby library (which is always kept locked when not in use) books have been found strewn around the floor on more than one occasion. Tradition has it that a murder was committed in this room, and there is a large stain on the floor-boards which will not wash out, and may be blood.

It occured to Mr. Symons that if he could find a way of getting rid of the stain, he might be rid of the haunting, and since it would not clean off he suggested to Mr. Eddy that they demolish the old floor and lay a new one, but the carpenter would not hear of it. 'Much better left alone,' was his comment, 'the old floor is still in fine condition, and I couldn't find you boards of that quality today.' So they compromised. The sinister stain was covered with a layer of plywood, which is of course hidden by the carpet. But the disturbances continue.

Mr. Symons finds it impossible to work in the library. If he remains there for any time the entire left side of his body drops to an abnormally low temperature, or appears to do so. The first time this happened he became concerned that he may have suffered a stroke, but to his surprise, when he touched the skin of his left arm it felt perfectly normal, yet the freezing sensation persisted. He described the symptoms to his doctor, who assured him, after a thorough probe, that all was in order, suggesting (and who can blame him) that his patient had imagined the whole thing.

At that time Mr. Symons was engaged in preparing a manuscript which necessitated lengthy spells in the library, but he found that the icy sensation, far from being imagined, was occurring more frequently and becoming an intolerable nuisance. He installed a powerful heater, and even then had to sit at his desk with a shawl draped round him in an attempt to halt the progressive refrigeration of his left side. Yet no other member of the household noticed the cold in the library, and in fact his father, who sometimes sat with him, complained only of the stifling heat. 'The ghost,' Mr. Symons says, 'just will not let me settle in there.'

But the most persistent evidence of a supernatural presence is the behaviour of the library door, which locks and unlocks on its own, sometimes imprisoning the unfortunate occupant for a time, then suddenly releasing him. A botanist friend was staying at the manor some years ago, and on the invitation of Mr. Symons' father had retired to the library one day for the purpose of writing up his latest field observations, but when he rose to leave he found the door locked against him. He became very alarmed, knowing that the house was at the time completely empty of people — even the staff were having a day off. Then without warning the door flew open, striking the unhappy visitor a violent blow in the face.

On the whole, the Treneere ghost is very much a conformist, displaying an all-too-familiar behaviour pattern. He turns lights on and off, locks and unlocks doors, throws things around, and is generally something of a prankster. Mr. Symons is on good terms with him despite having to remonstrate with him now and again when he becomes too obstreperous. The ghost dislikes being discussed (and how often have we been told this!) showing his displeasure in a number of ways. On the night following our visit he wrenched the handle off Mr. Symons' brass bedside lamp whilst the latter was reading in bed, by way of protest at our intrusion earlier in the day.

But are all these antics as frivolous as they seem? Are paranormal disturbances in reality a cry for help, a desperate attempt to draw our attention to the fearful dilemma of an earth-bound soul?

In the present case, the temptation to link cause and effect is hard to resist. Is the ghost a murder victim, or even the murderer himself? Or is he a fugitive from justice (or injustice), still emerging from his cramped hiding-place beneath the stairs to stretch his legs in the safety of the night? A simpler and less melodramatic possibility, that Treneere is haunted by a former owner can, I feel, be discounted if only on the ground that a past lord of the manor is unlikely to throw library books around and lock the door against one of his kin! Some ghosts show themselves, others do not, and since the Treneere ghost has been an entirely auditory phenomenen for at least a hundred years, any hope of identifying him seems very remote.

Over the centuries countless people must have lived or stayed at this extraordinary mansion, which gives the impression of having existed in a perpetual state of preparedness against some unspecified eventuality or other for most of its long life. Even the beautiful chapel, located — somewhat unusually — at the top of the house, has a kind of emergency exit from which one can reach the ground floor without recourse to the stairs, and in the huge loft a number of palliasses were discovered, clearly for the use of soldiery billeted there for some unrecorded reason.

But it is not an uneasy house. On the contrary, an atmosphere of calm restfulness informs the whole of this enchanting place, and if there are sometimes spirits abroad during the dark hours, such things are a very small part of the larger history which I hope will some day be written about Treneere Manor.

Chapter Five

'CURLEWS'

THE area known as Balnoon lies in a wide valley at the periphery of the villages of Lelant and Halsetown, and was itself a mining village long ago. The mine, further up on the Downs, bore the name 'Balnoon,' and since this is a Cornish word which translates as 'Mine on the Hill' one presumes the workings to have been in existence at a time when the Cornish language was still spoken, which makes it a very old mine indeed. Almost the only visible evidence of the village still remaining is the ruined chapel, seen in the grounds of Curlews Country Club.

Cornish historian Cyril Noall states that the lodes contained within this mine were rich but dangerous to work, held together as they were by a soft texture which rendered them liable to collapse easily.[1] In the year 1758 an accident of this sort occured, burying all the men working above and below ground,[2] and there have been intermittent reports of fatal accidents at the mine throughout the nineteenth century. It closed down finally in 1858, which means of course that it was actively worked for at least one hundred years and probably longer.

The large, somewhat rambling building known as 'Curlews,' now a club with restaurant, bars, billiard room and so on, was originally two separate buildings, one of which may have been the count-house serving Balnoon mine, although I have not been able to confirm this. Early in the nineteen-twenties the then owner, Miss Mary Richards, had the two buildings joined to make one large dwelling, which was purchased in 1924 by Miss L. E. Coward.

Miss Coward's nephew, the Newlyn sculptor Denis Mitchell, told me that he and his brother frequently stayed with their aunt at Curlews in those early years, and it was during one of these visits that there occured the earliest paranormal incident at the house of which I have any record. Miss Coward and the two boys were relaxing quietly in what I presume to have been the sitting-room one evening, when suddenly the marble clock on the mantlepiece began to rock from side to side like a marionette on a string. Mr. Mitchell assured me that the movement could not possibly have been caused by vibration from any exterior source such as wind or passing traffic. The night was still and quiet, besides which the sides of the clock were lifting as much as an inch off the shelf as the rocking continued.

Recognising that this was evidently a display of psychokinesis and of supernatural origin, Mr. Mitchell wondered if it might be associated with

[1]The St. Ives Mining District. Dyllanson Truran, 1982.
[2]William Borlase, 'Natural History of Cornwall'

31

the several fatalities which had occurred during the working life of the mine, the adit of which runs directly beneath Curlews, yet it seems that the ghost which has been troubling the building in recent years is that of a woman.

Soon after the affair of the dancing clock (but not, I understand because of it), Mr. Mitchell's brother began to try his hand at automatic writing. This commonly practiced form of mediumship consists of obtaining spirit messages by holding a pencil over a sheet of paper and allowing any spirit entities present to take control. But he soon found himself being 'taken over' by forces so malevolent and frightening that he quickly abandoned the experiment.

During the next quarter of a century Curlews changed hands several times, always remaining a private residence until the late nineteen-sixties, when it became an hotel. In 1974 however it was bought by Mr. Malcolm Legg and his wife Sue, who converted it into the licensed club which it still is. They told me that they remembered the departing hotelier warning them not to alter the place around 'or the little man who sits around smoking his pipe will come and haunt you.'

Naturally enough they treated this remark as a joke, but it was not long before they became aware of strange and unaccountable things going on. One night after they had closed up, they were climbing a flight of stairs which overlooked the lounge and bar, and both saw, at the same moment, a shadowy figure flit past the bar below them. They both knew they had seen a ghost, and were equally sure, by the clothing, that it was a woman.

As it turned out, a future proprietor saw the ghost in almost exactly the same spot a few years later, but Mr. Legg told me he always felt that the real focal point of the haunting was in one of the bedrooms above, where various supernatural events were reported including one memorable occasion when all the clothes were snatched from the bed by unseen hands at a time when it was occupied by two people enjoying a clandestine relationship!

Mr. D. S. Bramwell, a plumbing engineer who knew the building well, said that whenever he came to be working in the vicinity of the stairway, particularly near the landing, he fely uneasy, and although he saw nothing he was constantly aware of a 'presence.'

Sue Legg felt strongly that the influence was masculine rather than feminine, but my researchers have failed to reveal any reported sightings of the little pipe-smoking man, or for that matter any other male ghost.

At the time of writing, the owners of the club are Mr. Anthony Wadsworth and his wife Angela, who made a number of significant alterations to the place, since when there has been a steady crescendo of psychic activity, which, whilst seeming not to affect the smooth conduct of their business, must at times try both nerves and patience.

Two incidents were actually witnessed by customers dining in the restaurant. The first of these was when a quantity of glass sugar-shakers on a side table began to vibrate noisily, one of them then sailing through the air and landing in the middle of the floor, and on the second occasion a bottle rose from a shelf, remained suspended in the air for a second or two, then burst into fragments immediately behind where Mrs. Wadsworth chanced to be standing. 'The force of it,' she told me, 'laddered my stockings.' This comment seems to suggest that the bottle simply shattered as a result of hitting the ground from a height rather than from any paranormal agency, but witnesses saw it burst in mid-air. How the customers reacted to these unscheduled floor shows is not recorded!

The staff at the club have not escaped the attention of this intractable ghost. A waitress told me how, when she was stooping to pick up some bottles in a cellar behind the bar, a lemon shot up from a box full on the floor nearby, hitting her a blow on the chest. She said she was aware her assailant was the ghost, but added: 'She has done nothing like it since. I feel she is friendly towards me, and sometimes I see her, like a dark shadow, drift past me.'

A pile of clean towels left on the bar counter by the manageress was found on the floor, put back, and found again strewn around. Doors locked at night were found open in the morning without the aid of keys (a favourite parlour trick of ghosts by the way) and there is the inevitable tinkering about with the lights, so common with this type of haunting,* Mr. Wadsworth said that things reached a point when he could no longer persuade any of his staff, even with the inducement of a five pound bribe, to turn off the lights last thing at night and walk through the dark and deserted lounge.

He himself had his first actual sighting of the ghost when standing in the empty lounge and seeing the 'swirl' of a woman's skirt disappear round a corner of the bar. He went round to the back and called to his sister-in-law 'Brenda have you just been in the bar?' Then he noticed she was wearing slacks, not a dress. 'I went cold,' he admitted, 'because I knew then I had seen the ghost. Previously I had never believed in such things.

At this stage in our conversation, which took place in front of the bar where the ghost had been twice seen, Mr. Wadsworth broke off to complain of a 'tingling sensation' all over his body. The back of his hair rose, and 'goose pimples' appeared on his bared arms. My wife placed her hand on the side of his head and experienced what seemed like a mild electrical current passing through her fingers, and when I touched his arm I noticed the same sensation. This state of affairs lasted for about two minutes, then faded as abruptly as it had started.

Arguably, this condition was self-induced, nothing more than a *frisson* felt by Mr. Wadsworth in recounting his meeting with the ghost, but he assured me that only three hours previously he had stood in the same spot describing the same incident to another caller without experiencing any tingling or

*See remarks on this subject at the end of Chapter 6.

other sensation. Clearly bewildered and upset by this latest manifestation, he said he believed the ghost had come to remind him that she was 'still around.' If this was so, then it is the first time — to my knowledge — that a ghost has been present and 'listening in' to a conversation that directly concerned it!

All in all, there was by now enough evidence to confirm the existence of a genuine and sustained haunting at Curlews extending over many years, yet there have been periods in its history when no paranormal disturbances at all have occurred, or at any rate have not been reported. A well-known local businessman, the late Mr. Archie Dick and his wife lived there from 1949 till 1953, and were untroubled by supernatural phenomena of any kind. Their daughter Wendy, (Mrs. A. Guthrie) confirmed that it was an extremely happy period in her parents' lives, and she told me that they left only when Mr. Dick's health precluded him from any longer tending the huge garden which had been his hobby, and much of which is now, sadly, a car park.

It would seem therefore that this haunting is of the dormant variety, triggered off from time to time by the presence of someone in the house who acts unwittingly as a medium, attracting psychic elements as a magnet attracts metal.

As to the identity of the ghost, or ghosts, there is a persistent rumour of a woman and her baby having met their deaths in sinister circumstances in one of the upper rooms, but I have discovered no evidence to support such a story. However, at the close of the last century a young woman, said to have been pregnant, drowned herself in what came to be known as 'Liza's Pool' somewhere near to the mine. Today there is no sign of a pool, but it was probably the water collected and used by workers to operate the stamping machines during the summer months, when the natural streams tended to dry up. It is in fact recorded that there was a store of water for this purpose somewhere up there on the Downs.

Whether this unhappy woman lived in one of the two cottages which later became Curlews has to remain a matter for conjecture but the rumour of dark deeds within its walls doubtless stems from this episode.

Perhaps one day a fragment of history will surface to positively identify the Curlew ghosts. In the meantime the haunting continues, and indeed as I write these words news has reached me that the lady has again been seen.

Chapter Six

A HAUNTED LANE

ZENNOR, with its magnificent headland and its oddly fragmented village of Churchtown, is something of a showpiece in this part of Cornwall. By West Country standards the village itself hardly rates as a tourist attraction, but at least there is the fine old church from which the legendary mermaid lured her chorister to his doom in the waters below, and there is the popular 'Tinners' Arms pub, which, incidentally, has been haunted for as long as anybody can remember — but more of that later.

On the edge of the village, a narrow, twisting lane, much of it hidden by trees and shrubs, rises for about a mile in a south-easterly direction up to Foage farm alongside a fast running stream which has its origins somewhere in the hinterland beyond Foage. An idyllic place, one would have thought for a quiet, contemplative stroll.

However, Mr. and Mrs. Lawrey, who own the farm, have other things to say about this lane. Mrs. Lawrey told me that some people experience a sense of deep unease when walking in it, and one or two of the locals will not go near it.

Close to the farm, lying back a little from the lane, is a small, sturdy building which the Lawreys have skilfully converted into a pleasant cottage which they sometimes let to holidaymakers or to people awaiting more permanent homes in the area. Some of the lodgers have spoken of feeling a 'presence' in the cottage, and, interestingly, all these people describe the presence as 'friendly' and definitely female. Mrs. Lawrey herself is aware of a feeling of being watched when she stands in the cottage at times when it is untenanted, and now she will not go into it at all unless her dog accompanies her. Strangely enough the dog seems unaffected, but Mrs. Lawrey's horse could never be persuaded to pass the building, showing stress and panic when he was ridden towards it.

But there are other ghosts in the lane. A few weeks before I began my enquiries, Mrs. C. Somerville was standing in the garden outside her house in the village when a lady and gentleman approached her. After exchanging a few pleasantries the man said 'I expect you will think we're mad, but we believe we have just seen a ghost.' They had been enjoying a walk, they said, up the lane towards Foage farm when they were surprised to see a man dressed in Victorian working-man's clothes and riding an antiquated bicycle. As he sped past them they were horrified to see that blood was streaming down his face. Then: 'he seemed to vanish."

Although this startling apparition was seen within a short distance of the Lawreys' cottage with its ghostly 'presence,' it is difficult to see any obvious link between it and the violence and horror implicit in the fleeing cyclist. However, a fragment of history came my way later which offers at least a plausible explanation:

In the valley below the lane lie the remains of Rosevale tin mine, a sad wreck which has been ignored (or perhaps just overlooked) by nearly all local mining historians, despite the fact that it appears to have been worked over a much longer period of time than many of its contemporaries. In the lane above, now hidden from view by trees and a varied assortment of vegetation, are the remnants of cottages which almost certainly must have been the homes of some of the miners employed at Rosevale. Clearly then the lane had links with the mine, and there were probably access points leading down to it for the convenience of the workers.

In its long history only one accident has been reported from this mine, when a gas cylinder exploded,* shattering the face of one unfortunate fellow, who died later from his injuries. Did he, or some less severely hurt comrade, grab a bicycle and dash down to the village in search of medical help? Such a theory is not as fanciful as it may sound, for doctors were never in permanent attendance at the mines, and sometimes several hours elapsed before one could be located and brought to the scene of an accident.

At the 'Tinners' Arms' back in the village, successive proprietors have for many years been mystified by the sound of footsteps in an unoccupied room above the bar, heard when they have been clearing up after an evening's trade. One recent incumbent told me that his Alsatian dog, an unusually benign and friendly creature, glanced up at the bar ceiling on one of these occasions, bared his teeth in an angry snarl then fled from the building in terror.

Psychokinetic activity of a non-violent type occurs spasmodically. The present proprietor, Mr. David Care, told me that glasses, trays and other paraphernalia stacked away at night are sometimes found spread around the floor in the morning, but nothing is ever broken.

A former employee at the 'Tinners' made the interesting observation that phenomena at the Inn always seemed to occur before, during or after an electrical storm. If this smacks of melodrama we should remember that electricity is well-known to be a source of energy which promotes and encourages the paranormal. Poltergeists are invariably drawn to electrical installations wherever they are, causing lights to be turned on and off, bulbs to explode and electronically controlled apparatus to malfunction. Victorian authors of fictional ghost stories, whose moments of high drama so often included a raging tempest, may perhaps have recognised that the discharge of atmospheric electricity in some way attracts supernatural forces. Perhaps also, as science and psychic research draw closer together, physicists will one day be able to explain this strange affinity.

*Gas was introduced, as an overall lighting above and below ground, at many mines from the middle of the nineteenth-century, but candle-light was still extensively used by the miners individually. In such circumstances a stick of dynamite, carelessly handled, may have caused the Rosevale incident. Such details as I have been able to gather are sketchy and conflicting on this point. E.H.

Chapter Seven

GHOSTLY ST. IVES

ALTHOUGH ghosts are usually associated with old houses, castles and so on, they do in fact turn up in the most improbable places. Sightings have been reported on shipboard, in railway carriages, motor cars and aeroplanes. There is a haunting at London's Heathrow airport, and another on Covent Garden underground station.

Here in St. Ives a supernatural presence has been felt in Woolworth's stores, but the building is an old one formerly owned by a family draper, so that the ghost, if that is what it is, probably has connections with an earlier era.

A few years ago a particularly unpleasant ghost was seen at Clotworthys, the mens' outfitters in the High Street. The young assistant had opened up as usual one morning and was engaged in arranging some shelves behind the counter when he became aware of a sudden chill in the atmosphere. Turning round, he was horrified to see before him the figure of a man, or rather the lower half of a man, for the face seems not to have materialized despite the fact that the young man felt he was being glared at in a malevolent and thoroughly evil way. The figure then walked across the shop and up a flight of stairs which leads to the fitting-room, whereupon the terrified assistant fled the building and was given comfort and a stimulating drink in a nearby cafe.

Our local paper reported the affair and made some enquiries concerning the past history of the building, but nothing emerged to suggest who this belligerent phantom might have been, and as far as I am aware the matter was pursued no further.

A more genial spirit puts in an occasional appearance at the Regent Hotel in the upper part of St. Ives. This bright and pleasant building, which provides its guests with sensational panoramic views of the town and harbour from almost every window seems an unlikely place to encounter the supernatural, yet here he is, the ghost of a small, elderly and genteel man, dressed in nineteenth-century clothes and described by Mr. Keith Varnals, the proprietor, who has seen him twice, as probably belonging to the well-to-do middle-class of his time. The ghost has also been seen by at least two visitors but most frequently by a former chambermaid, who, far from being scared, came to regard the old gentleman as something of a pet. The focus of psychic activity seems to be centered in one of the upper rooms, but the ghost has been observed in a corridor and at the foot of the main stairway.

Nobody knows who he is, but part of the hotel was at one time a count-house serving the Pedn-Olva tin mine, and Mr. Varnals tells me that the ghost invariably turns up when any structural alterations to the hotel are in progress. Taking these two facts in conjunction, is the spectral visitor perhaps a mine superintendant searching for something hidden away in his old office? If so, structural upheaval would certainly excite him!

In an area conspicuous for eccentric street planning, it is perhaps not surprising to find two St. Ives roads, running parallel to one another, both bearing the name of Wesley Place. Patient scrutiny however reveals that where the house numbers end in one street they continue in the other. Surely the deliveryman's ultimate nightmare!

In 1976 Mrs. Rosemary Craze and her husband moved into one of these houses soon after their marriage. I cannot divulge which one since another family now occupies it, but it seems that the couple settled happily enough in it until one night Mrs. Craze awoke to see the door open and the figure of a man approach the bed. 'The room went very cold,' she told me, 'and I just sat up and stared. It took my breath away. I couldn't move or cry out to waken my husband.' She was able to observe and retain the details of his features and general appearance to an extent which is astonishing for a first sighting. 'I would say he was about seventy, wearing a peak cap and a mackintosh tied round the middle. Fairly stockily built, about five foot eight inches in height and a round, wrinkled face.'

When later she spoke of her ghostly visitor to some neighbours they told her the description fitted that of a man who had lived and died in the house. Mrs. Craze never actually saw him again, but he made his presence known in a number of ways. The front door would open and close, so also would an inner door and even the door of the room where they were sitting, followed by an indentation in an armchair or sofa, such as is made when a person sits. They came to joke about this, wondering if the ghost had come to watch television! Sometimes they would hear the back door open, and heavy footsteps ascending the stairs to the bedrooms. Naturally enough they always investigated, but there was never any sign of an intruder.

(It is interesting to note that the ghost was so frequently heard coming *into* the house, and that on the only occasion when Mrs. Craze saw him he was wearing a hat and raincoat. One might deduce from this that he was a constant visitor rather than a resident, but since this does not accord with the known facts there has to be some other explanation for this curious detail).

After the birth of Mrs. Craze's daughter Kelly the kindly old ghost seems to have interested himself in the child's welfare. Kelly slept in a room next to that occupied by her parents, and one night, hearing her crying, Mr. Craze got up to attend to her, but in the short time it took him to rouse himself and walk into the adjoining room the crying had stopped, and the cradle was gently rocking. At the time of this incident the child was two months old and could not possibly have activated the cradle herself.

A very unusual story, not without a certain puckish charm, was recounted to me by restaurateur Mr. John Bellaris, who bought an old count-house, once the property of the South Providence Mining Company in what is now Laity Lane in Carbis Bay. After they abandoned it, it became the home of Cornish author Charles Rodda, but when Mr. Bellaris took it over in 1976 it had been empty for some time, and consequently was in a bad state of repair.

The new owner set about having the place renovated and structurally altered to suit his requirements. 'Upstairs,' he told me, 'were three rooms, the centre one of which was always very cold, no matter what the temperature was like elsewhere in the building. Below, on the ground floor, we had to demolish the crumbling ceilings, which of course revealed the floor-boards above. To my astonishment, nailed to the floor beneath the middle room, was an old-fashioned bowler hat, one of those with a high crown, like Churchill used to wear.'

He removed the hat, placed it on a window sill and forgot it until some days later, when it dawned on him that the atmosphere in the upper middle room was no longer chilly. It had 'warmed up' to the temperature of the rest of the house. Then he noticed that the hat kept disappearing and turning up again in various places, and at first assumed his workmen were fooling about with it, but they assured him they had not touched it. However, to make quite sure he was not being made the target for a concerted leg-pull he tried placing the hat in a particular spot before leaving for the night, but when he returned in the morning ahead of his men it was always somwhere else. Finally one night he took it to the end of the garden and threw it out of sight behind some brambles. 'Nobody,' he emphasized, 'was around to see me do this.'

Next morning the hat was back in the house.

Mr. Bellaris had built a large fireplace, of the log-burning type, and beside it was a ledge on which he kept the hat, presumably as an antique curiosity. Inexplicably, the hat on one occasion fell into the flames, but when they retrieved it there was no sign of burn damage. Unable to believe what they were seeing, they tried applying a match to it, but it seemed to be fire-resistant, which, Mr. Bellaris admitted, 'really did scare us.' But apart from this incident the hat remained for most of the time on its ledge until he sold the property about four years after he had acquired it.

Then, on the night following the exchange of contracts, the hat vanished, and has not been seen since.

But that is not the whole story of the old count-house. The ghost of a small elderly man, seen in the house by several people at different times, used to come into the room where the new fireplace had been built, look around him and drift out again. On one occasion a guest called out 'John, who is the old boy leaning against the mantlepiece in your lounge?' Mr. Bellaris was quite sure who it was, but nevertheless gently led his friend into the lounge, where it was pointed out to him that there *was* no mantlpiece! It had been demolished to make way for the new fireplace. Evidently the visitor had entered a 'time-slip' situation, seeing the former occupant in an environment familiar to him during his earth life. There are in fact countless examples of these out-of-time experiences on record.

The reader cannot have failed to notice one or two striking points of similarity between this haunting and that at the Regent Hotel a mile or so down the road. Both buildings are former count-houses, both phantoms were small, oldish men, and their appearances were particularly noticeable during building alterations. Mr. Bellaris believes his ghost to have been a former mine official, and so do I. But the hat? Did it belong to the ghost, and why was it moved around so much, unless in a bid to attract attention? And why hide it beneath the floor? Possibly its discovery triggered off the haunting in the first place.

All we can be sure of is that the hat has gone. I do not know about the ghost.

The old 'Downlong' area of St. Ives, with its convoluted network of narrow, cobbled streets and alleyways should, one feels, be a ghost-hunter's paradise, and indeed many tales of the supernatural have survived for which unfortunately I have been unable to obtain back-up details, and which therefore must be regarded as suspect, or belonging to that category of hauntings too deeply rooted in the past for one to put together a reliable and coherent story.

However, a sensational and deeply disturbing incident occurred in the autumn of 1975 at the home of Mr. and Mrs. Anderson,* whose 200 years old cottage is one of the more attractive properties in 'Downlong.'

They were seated one Sunday evening in the lounge with two of their three children, reading and watching television. The third and youngest child, eight-years-old Pam, was playing by herself in a spare room above. 'Suddenly,' Mrs. Anderson told me, 'We heard the most awful scream, and dashed out in time to see Pam lurch across the landing, my son just managing to catch her before she fell down the stairs. Never have I seen a child in such a state of terror.'

They took her into the lounge and tried to calm her, but it was something like half-an-hour before they could get a word out of her, and when she did speak she simply said: 'The lady wants me.' Much later on, encouraged to say more about what had caused her so much distress, little Pam described how she had decided to join the family downstairs, but when reaching up to turn off the light-switch she felt strong arms gripping her from behind. 'The sister of the house had a little girl who died,' she told her parents, 'and she wants me instead.'

Mrs. Anderson said that this sentence, repeated over and over again, was all they could get out of their daughter, who, not surprisingly, refused to go

*At the behest of this lady and gentleman I have given them a pseudonym and concealed the precise location of their cottage. They tell me they may wish to sell it.—E.H.

upstairs again by herself, and for the rest of the winter slept in her parents' room.

During the ensuing weeks everything was done to divert the child's mind from the events of that Sunday evening by involving her in various activities away from the house, but these measures were only partially successful. Pam remained obdurate and totally withdrawn on the subject of her experience, and whereas Mrs. Anderson was sure her daughter had tangled with supernatural forces of some kind, her husband, who did not believe in such things, remained non-committal.

The affair might well have ended there, perhaps shrugged off as a childish fancy, had it not been for Mr. Anderson's involvement in a bizarre episode which contained a mixture of high drama and farce in the classic mould.

A property dealer by profession, Mr. Anderson was driving a couple of clients to his office at St. Ives, their route taking them along the Land's End road. I do not know the name of this couple, but for the purpose of this story I will refer to them as Mr. and Mrs. Smith. They were progressing at a leisurely pace until Mrs. Smith suddenly called out from the back 'Drive faster — the Revenue men are after us.' Uncertain as to whether he had heard aright Mr. Anderson stepped up his driving but Mrs. Smith yelled out: 'Faster, faster — they're catching us up.' The bemused driver pushed his foot down hard on the accelerator and they took off, but the Land's End road being what it is they could not maintain the pace and slewed to a halt. 'It's alright, don't worry,' called Mr. Smith, 'my wife is a medium. She sees things from the past.'*

Convinced by this time he was dealing with a pair of 'nutters,' Anderson got them to his office and plied them with mugs of coffee, but Mrs. Smith, who apologised for her behaviour in the car, spoke so convincingly of her mediumship that he finally became impressed by her obvious sincerity and told her of Pam's ordeal in the spare room. Could she employ her gifts to clear up the mystery?

The upshot of this was that Mrs. Smith spent an evening wandering through the rooms of the Andersons' cottage, presumably absorbing psychic impressions, then presented the family with a horrendous story.

A child of Pam's age had died there some time in the previous century. The 'sister of the house' referred to Pam was an elder sister whose unquiet spirit was suffering some feelings of guilt associated with her young sister's death — perhaps was inadvertently responsible for it — and wanted to replace her with Pam.

If we are to make any sense out of this, then by implication the elder sister is, or was, earthbound, and sought a physical replacement for her lost sister.

It has to be remembered that Mrs. Smith would have known the details of Pam's experience before the investigation, and could well have concocted

*Early in the last century Revenue officers, in conjunction with the army, were constantly engaged in rounding up bands of the smuggling fraternity operating in the coastal areas around Cornwall.—E.H.

this explanation to satisfy the parents. On the other hand a stray remark uttered by Pam herself some months later gives some credence to the story. She said to her mother, in almost the last reference she has ever made to the affair: 'That lady has gone now. She has stopped following me about because I'm nearly nine.'

In a further demonstration of her powers, which certainly seem to prove that she was a genuine psychic, Mrs. Smith asked if they were aware of the presence of a second ghost in the cottage. Mrs. Anderson said she was not surprised to learn this, as she had repeatedly heard footsteps pass her bedroom door at night and continue down the stairs. She had at first assumed that her son, whose room was on the floor above, was prowling about, but he assured her he had not left his bed, and soon the footsteps became a regular event, always occuring at the same time in the night.

Mrs. Smith asked whether, when they moved into the cottage, they had found any object left lying around by the previous occupant? Mrs. Anderson thought hard. There had been, she recalled, a little cross, fashioned out of straw, on a shelf in an upper room. It looked as if it had been there for a long time, and she had thrown it in the dustbin.

'You shouldn't have done that,' the medium told her. 'Try and find another one to put in its place.'

It happened to be around Easter time when this conversation took place, and Mrs. Anderson had no difficulty in procuring one of those little crosses made from palm-rush which churches distribute among their congregation. She placed it on the same shelf where the previous one had lain for so long.

The footsteps have not been heard since.

Chapter Eight

'IT WAS A BEAUTIFUL LADY'

GODOLPHIN HOUSE is located a mile or two inland from Mounts Bay, on the Kerrier-Penwith borders. Built at the time of Henry the Seventh it was the home of the Godolphin family for more than two hundred years, after which it passed to the fourth Duke of Leeds in whose family it remained right up until 1921. For some years after that it seems to have been occupied by farming families, but in 1937 the property was acquired by Mr. and Mrs. S. E. Schofield, who have done a great deal towards restoring the house to something like its former splendour, both inside and out.

The Godolphins were a remarkable lot. Francis (1536-1608) was a mining expert who made a fortune out of tin, the revenue from his various mines earning him a knighthood. Another member, Sidney, killed when fighting with the king's forces during the civil war, was a distinguished poet. But the most politically successful was another Sidney (1645-1712) who began his career as M.P. for Helston, went on to become First Lord of the Treasury and was made an earl in 1706.

Some years before reaching this exalted position, probably about 1668 when he was still in his twenties and serving the king as special envoy in France and Belgium, Sidney met and became engaged to a young maid of honour at the court of Whitehall by the name of Margaret Blagge.

There are two portraits of her in existence. One, by Mathew Dixon, tells us nothing, but the other one by Mary Beale shows an attractive, serene face framed by a mass of dark, curly hair reaching to her shoulders. She was a deeply religious girl, regarded at court as something of a saint, and for this reason she attracted the attention of John Evelyn the famous diarist, himself an extremely devout man. Evelyn, who moved freely in court circles, became a kind of tutelary diety in Margaret's life, frequently visiting her at her Whitehall chambers, where he instructed her in religious matters, after which they would kneel and pray together for hours at a stretch.

Whilst there is nothing in the voluminous correspondence which they exchanged over the years to suggest that this was anything more than a purely platonic friendship born out of a desire to serve God in their various ways, it is difficult to believe that Evelyn's interest in pretty Margaret was confined to her spiritual welfare. He seems to have deliberately steered her away from marriage with Godolphin indirectly by extolling the virtues of spiritual friendship as against temporal love and physical passion. They formed a pact of eternal friendship, doubtless initiated by Evelyn, who drew a picture of a kind of altar surmounted by a circle of five-pointed stars, calling it a 'symbol of inviolable friendship' which he pushed across to Margaret for her to append her signature.

We may perhaps wonder why Godolphin, who knew exactly what was going on, did not send this pious bore packing, but since Evelyn was a middle-aged man with a wife and family he could hardly have posed much of a threat to Godolphin, or indeed to Margaret, who despite her lack of sophistication was nobody's fool.

Nevertheless, there came a period when, coming ever more under Evelyn's influence she renounced Godolphin and marriage with the avowed intention of spending the rest of her life in religious meditation and solitude. With this purpose in mind she left the service of the king and took up residence at the home of Lord and Lady Berkeley, ostensibly to get away from the noise and bustle of the court, but more likely to avoid bumping into Godolphin. Evelyn naturally was delighted with this development and began visiting Margaret at her new chambers, but he was soon in for a disappointment.

It may have been Lady Berkeley who persuaded Margaret that she had made the wrong decision, or perhaps Margaret herself came to the conclusion that she was not after all cut out for the life of a religious recluse, because she began to slip away for meetings with Godolphin, and in the spring of 1675 they were secretly married. The Evelyn stronghold was broken.

Why it should have been so important to keep the marriage a secret from Evelyn is hard to understand, but this seems to have been Margaret's idea. Saint or no saint, history reveals a devious element in her nature.

In the meantime Godolphin went off the Holland on his king's affairs and the unsuspecting Evelyn continued calling on Margaret for prayers and meditation. It was almost a year before he found out about the marriage, and when he did he was, not surprisingly, angry and deeply hurt at Margaret's deception. Later however we find him reconciled and helping the couple to furnish their new home near Whitehall, at the same time offering Margaret advice in the matter of choosing servants, what herbs to keep in the house for medicinal purposes and a host of other domestic trivia which doubtless she could have adequately dealt with on her own. The truth was he could not let go.

Inevitably of course the prayer meetings and the correspondence tailed off until they finally ceased altogether, which must have been a great relief to the long-suffering Godolphin.

At the beginning of September 1678 Margaret gave birth to a son,* but she herself died a few days afterwards, apparently from puerperal fever. She had asked, either in a will or in a letter written just before her death, to be

*Francis, second and last Earl of Godolphin.

buried at Breage church in Cornwall (a few miles from Godolphin House) where her husband's forebears lay, adding that she wanted no costly funeral or tombstone over her grave.

It took fourteen days to convey the coffin containing her body from London to Cornwall, accompanied by a cortège of forty attendants, and according to some accounts Evelyn travelled down with the cortège, Godolphin following later in his own coach. But Evelyn, in his diary, categorically states that he accompanied the procession only as far as Hounslow, then turned round and went back to London, where he and Godolphin sorted through Margaret's letters and papers.

One can hazard a pretty shrewd guess as to why he wanted to share in that task, but why Godolphin, described as being 'grief-stricken' by his wife's death, failed to attend her funeral is beyond comprehension. Thus, the only two men in her short life who claimed her love and respect in their different ways both abandoned her when she came to make her last sad journey.

Her tomb is beneath the Godolphin chapel in Breage church, but the most poignant relic of this strangely moving story is a small copper plaque fixed to the base of the alter and said to have been removed from her coffin. Engraved upon it, almost certainly by Evelyn himself, whose many skills included line engraving, is Margaret's name and a short epitaph in Latin, beneath which he has cut a five-pointed star, his emblem of 'inviolable friendship.'

So, in the end, John Evelyn had the last word.

——————————

IN the autumn of 1950 Mr. and Mrs. Schofield were preparing to take their two sons back to school in Dorset at the end of the summer holidays, leaving their three-year old daughter Elizabeth at home in the care of her Nanny for the one night they expected to be away. At the last moment however this much cherished nurse had to rush off in order to sort out some family crisis of her own, her place being taken by two good friends of the Schofields, a Group Captain Payne and his wife Hilda, who volunteered to spend the night at Godolphin House in order to look after the little girl. It was arranged for Mrs. Payne to share a room with Elizabeth (Mrs. Schofield's room in fact) while the Group Captain, a dedicated and prolific snorer, was parked in a room at the end of the corridor, out of earshot.

At some time in the night — the precise hour is unrecorded — Elizabeth called out 'Auntie Hilda, please put your light on.' She then ran across to Mrs. Payne's bed and dived into it saying 'I've just seen a white lady standing by my bed and I'm very frightened.'

Mrs. Payne, by nature a very nervous woman, reacted to this alarming piece of news by joining her small room-mate under the bed clothes, where they remained for the rest of the night. In the comforting light of day however, Mr. and Mrs. Payne came to the conclusion that Elizabeth had been dreaming of her departed Nanny, to whom she was passionately devoted, but Elizabeth, who seems to have been a remarkably articulate child for her age, indignantly refuted this suggestion. 'It wasn't Nanny,' she protested, 'it was a beautiful lady with black curls down to here—,' indicating her shoulders. This is a fair description of Margaret Blagge. Then she startled them by adding 'she went PUFF out of Mummy's cupboard.' In other words, the ghost came out of, or went into, Mrs. Schofield's wardrobe.

When later in the day her astonished parents learned of these events, Mr. Schofield recalled seeing an early plan of the house which showed that the original door to Mrs. Schofield's room was *immediately behind where the cupboard now stands.* The door led to a wing of the house long since demolished.

This seems to confirm that little Elizabeth witnessed a genuine psychic phenomenon. Mrs. Schofield told me she had always understood, from previous owners, that the place was haunted by a 'white lady' although she herself had not seen the ghost. In the gardens at the eastern end of the house is a wide pathway known as the 'ghost walk,' where Margaret Blagge is supposed to walk on each anniversary of her funeral, although personally I am more than a little wary of tales about ghosts who appear on anniversaries. They are, like ghosts who appear at midnight, something of a cliché. But Mrs. Schofield says that a little chapel formerly stood at the end of this pathway, of which only the arched entry still stands, so it is not impossible that Margaret's body was taken there pending the completion of funeral arrangements over at Breage.

Reading W. G. Hiscock's 'John Evelyn and Mrs. Godolphin,'* I was particularly struck by an episode, trivial in itself, but which might conceivably be linked with the appearance of Margaret Blagge's ghost — if that is what it was — at Elizabeth's bedside.

One day in 1674, the year before her marriage, Margaret was asked by the Evelyns if she would look after their six-year-old daughter for a few days while they were away. Margaret, who loved children, was only too happy to do so, and Evelyn wrote her an effusive letter of thanks. Here is her reply to that letter, which I have thought advisable to 'edit' in the interests of those readers who may be unfamiliar with the spelling and muddlesome syntax of the period.

In essence the letter remains unaltered:
> '*You make so many excuses for so small a favour. I beseech you, let me hear no more on the subject. Bless us all, what a fuss about trusting me with this pretty child for a few days. You need not worry about her eating meat, for she told me she never eats any at night. Her supper last night was gooseberry tart! She has a great sense of humour. Her maid forgot her nightdress so she went to bed in one of*

*Macmillan & Co., 1951.

46

mine, which much amused her. The night being hot she threw off the clothes, which made her cough a little, but I covered her up and thank God she slept well. A thousand thanks to Mrs. Evelyn that she has trusted me with such a jewel. I pray to God that I may well discharge my trust, and so bless you both. Amen.'

The child's name was Elizabeth, although I suppose we should not attach too much significance to this curious coincidence.

There have been other ghosts at Godolphin House. A previous owner told Mrs. Schofield that a young servant girl in her employ suffered a severe fright when she entered the dining room early one morning and saw 'a gentleman in evening dress' standing by the fireplace looking at her. He promptly vanished. We do not know who he was, but the 'evening dress' was probably court dress of an earlier period.

Another manifestation observed several times by Mrs. Schofield herself is of special interest. One morning during the early 'fifties the family was seated at lunch in the morning-room, which overlooks the courtyard, when Mrs. Schofield's attention was caught by what appeared to be a man's face staring from the big central window of the King's room opposite. This large and beautiful apartment is so called because it is believed that Charles the Second, whilst still prince, stayed briefly in that part of the house en route for France at the time of his father's trial. For many years the room was used by farmers for the storage of wheat and grain, but upon receipt of a grant in 1957 the Schofields restored it to its original splendour.

The window is set in a recess or alcove, containing a wide shelf, and the figure, described by Mrs. Schofield as having a bright complexion, dark hair and short, pointed beard was resting his elbows on the shelf and looking out into the courtyard though not directly at the morning-room. She saw the face a number of times after that, always from the same window. Yet no one else did, and the family finally came to the conclusion that it was an optical illusion caused perhaps by the play of light on old and distorted glass, which explanation, however, does not cover the fact that Mrs. Schofield was the only member of the household to see it.

Later that year, when Godolphin House opened its doors to the public, Mrs. Schofield was showing a party of visitors around when the inevitable question was asked: 'Are there any ghosts?' She told them the legend of the 'white lady,' and for good measure added her own 'face at the window' experiences.

A few weeks later she received a letter from some people who had been in the party, enclosing a snapshot they had taken of the front of the house, with the query: 'is this your ghost?' Staring down from one of the bedroom windows, and immediately recognised by Mrs. Schofield, was the bearded face she had come to know so well.

Their son John, then a boy of twelve, slept in that particular room, which is in the private section of the house and barred from visitors, so that it is inconceivable that anyone could have been in it, but the Schofields did check to see if some object in the room such as a painting on the wall could have produced the illusion of a face from the ground below, but they discovered nothing.

Ultimate confirmation that the face was a supernatural phenomenon came from an unexpected quarter. The County Archivist had lent Mr. Schofield some papers written by the Reverend Rundle, vicar of Godolphin church* from 1879 to 1906. They were historical notes concerning Godolphin House, and contained this passage: 'Previous owners have reported seeing a man's face looking out of the middle window of the king's room.'

*No connection with Godolphin House.

Chapter Nine

THE PHILLACK HAUNTING

FOR most tourists, Hayle is just a place one drives through to reach Penzance or St. Ives. However, if not in one of Cornwall's more salubrious areas it has nevertheless played an immense part in the County's industrial history, as a result of which by the middle of the nineteenth century the population had quadrupled. One unhappy outcome of this was that the twelfth century Phillack church, built on a hillside overlooking Hayle, was almost entirely scrapped and rebuilt to accommodate the big increase in the number of worshippers, although a few fragments of the original building remain, including the splendid fifteenth century tower.

Mr. Jack Hughes was born and grew up in Hayle. Once a time-serving soldier he travelled a great deal of the world, but he lives now quietly in his native town where he is gaining a wide reputation for his powers as a psychic healer.

Many years ago — Mr. Hughes thinks he could have been about sixteen at the time — he and his father were walking home late one night after visiting friends in a village beyond Phillack which bears the improbable name of Mexico. They had rounded the steep bend past Phillack church and were trudging the last few hundred yards down Lethlean-lane into Hayle when they heard footsteps approaching them. 'We aren't the only ones out late tonight,' remarked Hughes senior, and they looked to see who was about to pass them. But they saw no one. Instead, as the footsteps drew level, a cold draught of air hit them 'with a swishing sound,' and the pair of them took to their heels, running 'as fast as our legs could carry us' down to Hayle, home and safety.

Tangible evidence that this particular stretch of road down from Phillack was haunted came to light as time went on. Listening to a conversation between two young men in his local pub, Jack Hughes was surprised to hear one of them telling the other how his father had heard footsteps late one night and felt a draught of cold air in his face at what seemed to be the same spot.

Later still, two men, acquaintances of Mr. Hughes, were walking their dogs *up* the hill one evening when the dogs suddenly stopped and refused to budge, growling and staring ahead of them with hackles raised. Persuasion having failed the men finally picked the two pooches up and pressed on, bearing them in their arms, but when they reached the bend both animals struggled to be released and bounded happily on ahead.

It is clear that some kind of powerful supernatural force was active along this piece of roadway, and some interesting facts emerged during the course of my enquiries.

Mr. Hughes told me that when he was a boy an old thatched cottage stood by the side of the road here, long since demolished to make way for a housing estate, but on the opposite side there still remains an old gateway leading to a farm. It appears that this farm, or at least the land, was owned by one Canon Hockin, rector of Phillack from 1853 to 1902, a very long incumbency for those days. The venerable gentleman in fact owned a great deal of land around Phillack, receiving fat dues from the mines being worked on his property. Wheal Lucy tin mine on Black Cliff was named after his daughter, and the so-called 'Boiling Well' mine on Upton Towans, which contained a rich lode of silver lead, actually ran under the church itself.

A story concerning this busy cleric, which tends to confirm the feeling that he must have been a man of some wealth, is that a stone bridge which spans the river below Phillack was heightened on his instructions to facilitate the passage of his own boat. It is probably true, for I have had a look at this bridge, and one of the two arches is considerably higher than the other. It would be interesting to know what purpose the boat served, since it is difficult to believe that the Canon sailed up and down this unattractive stretch of water just to admire the view.

His ghost, wearing a black cloak, is allegedly seen crossing the road from the Rectory to the church, but only when the Rectory is vacant, which presumably means the interval between the demise or retirement of one rector and the installation of the next. If this is true his appearances must obviously be very infrequent.

But what of the footsteps further down the hill which scared Jack Hughes and others? Was this also the unquiet spirit of Canon Hockin, still pacing around the Parish he served for so long, searching for the long vanished mines which helped him prosper?

Perhaps, though I am more inclined to believe this to be a different and unassociated haunting, for the behaviour of the two dogs showed that there was an area of psychic disturbance which began near the farm gate and ended about one hundred yards further up the hill. The solitary thatched cottage mentioned by Mr. Hughes could have been the key to this strange business, but it has gone for ever, and so probably has the unseen ghost, for as far as I know there have been no reports in recent years of supernatural happenings in Lethlean-lane.

Chapter Ten

'THE FIRST & LAST GENTLEMAN'S HOUSE

ABOUT five miles out of Helston on the Lizard road, in what surely must be one of the most attractive wooded areas in all West Cornwall, stands the ancient manor house of Bochym.

At the time of the Domesday roll in 1087 this mansion was taxed in the name of 'Buchent,' being held by Robert, Count of Mortein, the half-brother of William the Conqueror, and there is living evidence of its existence at that time in the shape of a huge mulberry tree in the terraced gardens, known to be at least a thousand years old.

In Tudor times the family of Bochym were lords of the manor, but during the short reign of Edward the Sixth, John Bochym unwisely supported the Cornish rebellion which was crushed at Exeter in 1549, resulting in his arraignment on a charge of high treason. Inevitably it cost him his head and the sequestration of all his possessions and land to the Crown, but King Edward handed the property to one Reginald Mohun, Sheriff of Cornwall, so that it once more became a Cornish possession. During the Civil War it was a place of refuge for the Royalists, and there are, in the so-called 'Oak Room' (now a restaurant), sliding panels in the wainscot and a secret stairway which I have seen and enjoyed the privilege of ascending! Early in the nineteenth-century the building was thoroughly renovated and added to by Richard Davey in accordance with plans and elevations found among family papers, and it now occupies three sides of a square with a central north-facing wing. The house is panelled throughout, the library in Italian walnut, the dining-room in oak, and there are marvellous, intricate carvings on some of the walls.

The estate is owned by Major John Bradley, but the mansion has been leased to Mrs. Peggy-Anne Prowse, who conducts the affairs of the restaurant with her partner Mrs. Elizabeth Trapp.

Odd as it may seem, the only ghost inhabiting this history-soaked place is not, as one might suppose, some swash-buckling cavalier or headless Bochym, but a woman. Known for many years as 'The Pink Lady,'* she indicates her presence almost daily in a variety of ways, although the last actual sighting was in the nineteen-seventies, when a young boy saw her cross the floor of his bedroom. He recalled that the top of her head was level with the transom, or central division of the window, so that by measuring the distance from there to the floor Major Bradley was able to establish that the

*By a remarkable coincidence, a ghost also referred to as 'The Pink Lady' haunts No. 10, Downing Street. Among people to have seen her is former prime minister Harold Wilson, now Lord Wilson.—E.H.

51

ghost is four feet ten inches in height, which makes her either a very small lady indeed or, as I suspect, a young adolescent.

'I have not seen her,' Mrs. Prowse told me, 'but whenever we make up a bed in the suite she is supposed to have occupied, we return to find a dent in it such as would be left if somebody had been sitting on it.' Cutlery on the restaurant tables gets shifted around when no-one is present, and a tall door leading to an anti-room at the inner end of the restaurant, kept bolted when not in use, will at times rattle and shake in a most eerie fashion. (Incidentally, the entrance to the secret stairway is in this anti-room, which leads to the Pink Lady's suite).

The chef, Mr. Stephen Phillips, described how on one occasion he was stooping over his stove in the kitchens when he was dealt a painful blow on the back of his neck. He jumped round to identify his assailant but there was no-one about. The blow, he told me, raised a weal which lasted quite some time. Another curious incident involved Mrs. Prowse. 'I had gone behind the bar,' she said, 'and I thought some of the glasses looked a bit dusty, making a mental note to ask Frank our barman to give them a polish. I then went off to another part of the house on some errand or other, and when I returned to the bar a few minutes later the barman was standing there white as a sheet. I asked him what was the matter and he said the glasses on the shelf had just jumped off at him. None of them broke. It seemed that the ghost had picked up my thoughts.'

Cornish born Mrs. Prowse claims to be a descendant of the celebrated Trelawny family, who owned Bochym for a while,* and she feels a sense of deep identity with the house. 'When first I walked in,' she told me, 'I felt I knew where each room was.' She believes this to be inherited memory, a theory now widely accepted by Parapsychologists to account for the belief expressed by some people that they recognize a particular place or building 'from a previous incarnation.'

Neither she, her husband or their three children find the Pink Lady in the least bit frightening, and in fact the ghost has shown herself to be favourably disposed towards Mrs. Prowse. Her co-proprietor Mrs. Trapp has twice been violently thrown forward by some psycho-activated force, the Chef as we have seen was hit on the neck, and the barman had his glassware thrown around, but Mrs. Prowse had not so far been physically assaulted by this somewhat unpredictable lady!

The paranormal movement of various objects around the house is almost commonplace. Chairs are seen to move, light switches are turned on and off and so on, incidents witnessed not only by Mrs. Prowse but also by members of her staff. As is often the case with hauntings of long standing, no-one has been able positively to identify the Pink Lady, nor why she is so-called. The obvious inference, that she always appears wearing a pink dress, raises interesting speculation. Was it a favourite dress? Or was she wearing it when

*The property was in fact bought by Sir Humphrey Trelawny, Bart., in 1785.—E.H.

she met her death? Legend has it that she took her own life after her lover had been killed in a duel with her father, but if there is any substance at all in this story one would expect her identity to be known or at least guessed at.

However, true or false, it leads us to examine the terrifying supernatural episode witnessed by sub-Lieutenant A. Jelf, R.N., who was stationed at the Balloon Corps base about a mile to the East of Bochym during the first World War.

The incident is graphically described in two letters. One written by Jelf himself, the other by a resident of Mullion by the name of Miss McKean, with whom Jelf appears to have been billeted. The circumstances surrounding these letters, how and why they came to be written, are somewhat confusing, but I believe the sequence of events to be as follows:

A gentleman by the name of Williams, living then in the village of Lanarth a few miles from Bochym, evidently came to hear of sub-lieutenant Jelf's experience and wrote to Miss McKean for more precise details. By now the war had been over for more than a year, but Miss McKean managed to get in touch with Jelf, who duly replied to Mr. Williams but sent his reply to Miss McKean, presumably to check the story for accuracy. She then sent the letter to Mr. Williams with a covering letter adding her own comments. At a later date Williams sent the letters — or copies of them — to Cornish historian Charles Henderson for inclusion in the latter's notes on Bochym. Henderson died in 1933 and the bulk of his unpublished material was transferred to Truro museum, where curator Mr. H. L. Douch, after diligent search, succeeded in unearthing the two letters for me.

Here is the text of sub-lieutenant Jelf's letter, dated 17th April, 1919:

I am very sorry not to have replied to your letter before but I have been away for some weeks and have only just received it. The experience I went through took place on Oct. 15th 1917, so that I may be incorrect as to detail but the main story is as follows.

I was walking into Mullion from Cury Cross Lanes at about 7.30 or 7.45. It was a clear bright starlight night and the air was so pure that I was drinking in the sweetness of the hedgerows rather than preoccupied with my thoughts. As I was ascending the hill on the Mullion side of the Bochym valley I was gripped with a sudden intense fear akin to panic and stopped dead. I felt that I had to look up and beyond the trees on the right of the road I saw through a gate two figures engaged in a duel with long swords or rapiers. They were distant about fifty yards yet I could clearly discern their attire, the one on the right wore knee breeches, a short dark green cloak and a white or light coloured ruff and a cap with a feather. I cannot remember anything about the other man except that he seemed to be in keeping with the first. I confess that I was too terrified to stir and watched. The duel lasted I should say between ¾ of a minute to 1½ though it is very difficult to judge accurately of such incidents. Then one man on the left fell in such a way as to lead me to believe him killed. The other bent over him for a moment and then rose and beckoned with his hand to someone I could not see. After a few seconds there appeared from the inside of the hedge beyond the gate, where they had hitherto been hidden from my sight 6 men attired similarly to the principals in the duel. They were bearing a coffin which they rested beside the stricken man. The victor of the combat raised his hand and I imagined that he was pointing at me – at any rate I am sorry to say that I lost what little nerve was left me and the next thing I remember waking up in the road. All signs of the strange figures had disappeared. I made my way to Mullion very much shaken, and it was weeks before I could be persuaded to pass that way again. A month or two later I was content to assume that it was some kind of waking dream caused by bad digestion or strain – the result of considerable flying. Lately however I have been thinking it over and I have found one or two points rather difficult to reconcile with that theory. One is that no dream of the usually accepted type could cause a person not only to faint but to carry with him for some weeks a sense of terror. Up till then I had been an absolute sceptic with regard to psychic phenomena of any sort and I was not in any way a nervous kind of person. I have been in one or two more or less tight places without feeling in any way the extreme panic which took hold of me on this occasion. Finally I did not know at the time the existence of the old house of Bochym. One normally seeks in other cases for explanations which fit in with the known laws of nature, yet it seems to be as well to investigate them from other points of view and I am willing to believe that my vision may have been caused by some action of my subjective or subconscious mind acted upon by telepathy from someone else whose subconscious mind was aware of this duel or knowledge of it inherited in my own. I should be very grateful Sir, if you would let me know of any such duel having taken place in the past.

Miss McKean's 'back up' letter adds little of importance to this remarkable narrative, but is still worth quoting for other reasons, not the least being its stunning impact:

I enclose a letter from sub. lieut. A. Jelf, R.N. for you. I heard from him last night asking me to look over his statement of his ghostly encounter at Bochym. He was on his way to my bungalow when it happened and I was the first to be told about it. He arrived about 8.30 p.m. in a terrible state and covered with mud. I thought first he had fallen out of the car which usually brought the men down from the air station. By degrees he told me what had happened. He seems to have run most of the way from Bochym, a long way if you know where the Polurrian Hotel is, my bungalow is next to it. I think his letter is quite correct but somewhat bald. As he related it to me at the time it seemed more dramatic. The duellist who killed the other as he

*raised himself from looking at his fallen foe slowly turned and
pointed his sword at Mr. Jelf as the men brought the coffin towards
the dead man is what he told me at the time, and then he fainted and
can't remember how long he lay on the ground. The roads were
muddy though the night was fine and there was no moon and a dark
night except for stars. I may add Mr. Jelf went through the Battle of
Jutland and has done a great deal of flying. I consider him distinctly
psychic, for as a boy he told me he slept in a room where he felt a
presence but saw nothing and the room turned out to be haunted. I
have often urged him to send his Bochym experience to the Psychical
Society but he was afraid to! You are the first I know to whom he has
written it. I am most anxious to know if that duel was in any way
connected with the girl who haunts Bochym. I don't know the family
and have no information on the subject. It would be interesting to
know if a duel was fought on October 15th at any period at Bochym
especially that of Charles the first or earlier.*

Miss McKean undoubtedly heightens the drama for us. One can see the
young officer straggering across the threshold, exhausted and covered with
mud, blurting his story out bit by bit. Her memory is impressive. She
corrects a detail from Jelf's written account of the affair, and is even able to
recall what the weather was 'fine and there was no moon and a dark night
except for stars.' Jelf does not say if the moon was shining but states that it
was a 'clear bright starlight night,' which seems to confirm that there was no
moon, yet, standing at an estimated distance of fifty yards from the
combatants, he could describe the manner of their dress in detail, including
the colour.

It is this apparent anomaly which provided a clue as to what really
happened to airman Jelf that night. I think he comes near to the truth
himself when he says 'my vision may have been caused by some action from
my subjective or subconscious mind.' More precisely, he entered a 'time
distortion' situation, witnessing subjectively an event which took place on
that spot a couple of centuries earlier, and which probably continues to be
seen under certain climatic conditions and in the presence of anyone with
with psychic gifts, which according to Miss McKean the young officer
possessed.

Was this the duel fought between the Pink Lady's lover and her father?
Major Bradley tells me that the lover is reputed to have been a servant in her
father's house, in which case we can dismiss any such speculation, since no
lord of the manor would demean himself by fighting a duel with one of his
own servants. There would have been less ostentatious ways of dealing with
him!

There is in fact no reason for assuming that Jelf's vision was connected
with the Bochym haunting. After all, duelling was a common enough way of
settling disputes in past centuries, and I suspect that Bochym has had its

share of them.

Miss McKean's bungalow, by the way, still stands. I found it easily enough thanks to her own incidental reference to its location, but the present occupants, Mr. and Mrs. D. G. Oake from London understandably knew little of its more distant history. Mrs. Oake, however, told me of a gentleman named Gordon Gilbert, now in his eighties, who has lived all his life in Mullion and knew the bungalow well. She promised to contact him, and a day or two later telephoned me to say that Mr. Gilbert remembered his late wife telling him about the Jelf incident, and that a friend of hers, a Mrs. Baker, had actually been in the bungalow on a visit when the terrified young officer burst in with his story. Thus has been established a tenuous link with the events of that October night sixty-five years ago.

I suppose it is just possible that Mr. Jelf is still alive, but I know nothing about him or his whereabouts, nor does there seem any point in seeking him out. His letter says it all.

A final word about Bochym manor house. Somebody in the last century dubbed it 'The First and Last Gentleman's House in England,' which may raise a few eyebrows, but which I am sure is just a harmless reference to its position on the map!

Chapter Eleven

THE STROKING GHOST

CORNISH historian Cyril Noall wrote that Kenegie manor had been 'one of the most haunted houses in Cornwall.' The local peasantry, it seems, had for generations babbled on about the spectral horrors within its walls, and Victorian writer William Bottrell went so far as to concoct a highly romanticised and largely fictional account of the ghosts which were supposed to haunt it.

Like so many ancient seats around the County, Kenegie's history stretches back to mediaeval times, but the earliest reliable evidence of occupancy dates from the middle of the sixteenth-century, when it was owned by the family of Tripcony. A John Tripcony was vicar of nearby Gulval church in 1570.

Towards the end of the century it became the property of one Arthur Harris, who in 1596 obtained the coveted post of 'Captain of the Mount,' which meant in effect he was in charge of a small corps of the militia permanently garrisoned over at St. Michael's Mount. In his old age he handed the Kenegie estate over to his elder son William, a profligate and spendthrift whose only recorded act of any merit took place during the Civil War, when he courageously supported the King's cause, a loyal gesture which cost him a fine of £250.

On William's death Kenegie passed to his brother Christopher, but the family becoming extinct in the male line in 1775 the estate went to William Arundell, a member of the well-known and widely dispersed family of that name. Next we find it occupied by farmers, but then an eminent London surgeon by the name of Coulson, who later became Sheriff of Cornwall, bought the place and held it until 1866, when it was acquired by a branch of the Bolitho family in whose possession it remained until the nineteen-twenties. For many years now it has been an hotel, and is currently owned by Mr. Michael Vernon and Mr. Chris Cocklin. Happily both men have an obvious affection for the fine old mansion and an abiding interest in every aspect of its long history, so that at least one can be sure that after a period of well-nigh catastrophic neglect and dereliction Kenegie is once more in good hands.

And what about the ghosts?

According to Bottrell, the mansion had for a time been haunted by the noisy and boisterous ghost of a housekeeper formerly in the employ of the Harris family. Wondering if this individual had really existed or if she had been a product of Bottrell's fertile imagination, I asked Mr. Cocklin about her, and he told me that two of his guests, neither of whom had any knowledge of Kenegie history, had on separate occasions entered the lounge and seen the figure of a tall woman in a long black satin dress and a girdle around her waist from which dangled a bunch of keys. Both descriptions tallied precisely.

Mr. Cocklin has not seen this apparition, but he does have curious evidence of a supernatural presence in this same spacious room, which was probably the dining-hall in former times. A reproduction painting of Elizabeth the First used to hang on the wall until they discovered that, no matter how straight they hung it, they would later find it tilted to an angle of some ten degrees. Obviously they looked for some natural explanation, but finding none they came to the conclusion that the ghost was responsible. They removed the portrait and replaced it with one of Henry the Eighth. The tilting ceased completely, then started up again when they experimentally returned the Queen's picture.

Another visitor, who knew nothing of these events, spoke of feeling a powerful feminine presence in the lounge coupled with the impression that it was someone who hated other women. This hardly makes her unique, but, as Mr. Cocklin pointed out, might explain her antipathy towards the painting of Elizabeth!

Elsewhere in the house supernatural happenings are frequent and varied. Barman Mr. Ian Green told me he was seated at a table writing in what is called the 'Tudor' bar one day during an off-duty period. The bar was closed, no one apart from himself being in the room. Something made him turn round, and he saw the figure of a man dressed in brown — he recalled no other detail about the clothes — standing by the fireplace. Mr. Green looked away and continued his writing, then turned again. The figure was still there. Three times he turned to see the figure standing in the same spot, but when he looked a fourth time it had vanished. 'In matters supernatural,' he said to me, 'I have an open mind. I can only tell you what I saw.'

From another room Mr. Cocklin and most of his staff often hear the sound of voices, as though several people were engaged in conversation. At first they used to investigate, only to find the room empty, but the event has now become commonplace enough for them to accept the voices as some kind of psychic phenomenon.* Interestingly, the voices are heard only outside the room, never from the inside.

In the kitchens, a rather more specific sound is occasionally heard — that of a girl laughing. A maintenance engineer, working alone there and suddenly hearing the laughter, described it very concisely: 'not a woman, not a child, but a young girl.' I am assured, by the way, that no female member of the staff is around when this intriguing sound is heard, thereby eliminating the most obvious explanation!

*Bottrell mentions the same phenomenon, except that in his version the voices emanate from a summer-house in the grounds.—E.H.

There is the usual irritating and at times even dangerous ghostly fooling around with electric light switches, water taps, stoves and so on. Mr. Cocklin told me that on one occasion the water supply failed when an important function was in progress, and that after frantic searching they discovered that a stop-cock, *totally inaccessible except by removing the floor boards,* had been turned off.

Finally, I listened to a remarkable story of 'tactile' haunting, that is, actual physical contact with a ghost.

The details were provided by Mr. Cocklin's wife Shirley.

'When we came here, the place was derelict,' she said, 'and we were working round the clock to try and get it ready for opening as quickly as possible. One day I felt so exhausted that I went up to my room, undressed and got into bed. I think it was still daylight, but I am not sure. I must have drifted off to sleep because I remember waking up and seeing the door opening, then somebody or something came up to me and stroked my face, with the back of the hand, from my mouth to my ear. Then I imagine I turned over and went back to sleep. I gave the matter no further thought, thinking that perhaps Chris had come into the room to see if I was asleep then gone out again.'

But a few days later she was talking with some villagers from Gulval, who brought up the subject of hauntings in the mansion. One of them surprised her by saying 'then there's the Stroking Ghost who goes about stroking faces.' Asked what she meant, the woman placed her fingers to the side of her mouth and drew them up to her ear. 'It always strokes like that, in an upward movement.'

Mrs. Cocklin then remembered her own experience. They later found out that during the war, when the mansion had been requisitioned by the Land Army, several of the girls billeted there had experienced the Stroking Ghost's ministrations. It was always the same story: a light, finger-tip pressure from mouth to ear, with the back of the hand.

This extraordinary story at first suggests that Kenegie is harbouring, among its many spooks, an amorous male who enjoys stroking women's faces. But I think we may be doing this gentle ghost an injustice, for the stroking action seems soothing rather than sensual. Mrs. Shirley Cocklin, exhausted from overwork, rather confirms this impression. 'I imagine I turned over and went back to sleep.' A healing gesture?

Chapter Twelve

THE DOOR THAT WILL NOT STAY SHUT

LOOKING across the Rosemorran valley from Kenegie one can just make out the long thatched roof of Rosemorran Manor, surely one of the most beautiful farmhouses in Cornwall.

There is an interesting link between the two houses of Kenegie and Rosemorran, for George John of the latter house married the eldest daughter of William Arundell of Kenegie* some time late in the eighteenth-century, and it is a matter for regret that not one jot of information survives to tell us something about this union, which for a time linked the two estates.

I talked to the present owners of Rosemorran, Mr. and Mrs. J. S. Rodda, and asked them if they were aware of any supernatural activity in or around their elegant home. Mr. Rodda, who was born nearby and has known the farm and manor all his life, told me that the house is reputedly built on the site of a fourteenth-century monastery, and that one of his employees, Mrs. Sylvia Bodinar, had had a few experiences which tended to confirm this belief.

Mrs. Bodinar was busy in the huge greenhouse which runs parallel with the house, but she downed tools to come and talk to us. Twice she had seen what she described as a 'shapeless apparition' walking the length of the greenhouse, finally vanishing through the door at the end. The third and last time she saw it however, the figure assumed a more positive identity. 'It was wearing what looked like a black duffel-coat with the hood up,' she said, 'and this time instead of walking to the end of the greenhouse it turned off half way down and disappeared. I stood waiting for it to come back, but that was the last I saw of it.' Mr. Rodda told me that before the greenhouse was built there was a wall running along that section of the grounds with a door let into it, which led to a large rockery.

I think that Mrs. Boddinar may have seen the ghost of a Black Friar or Benedictine monk (the black habit could apply to either order) walking where perhaps in his time there was a cloister, or at least a regularly used route. But a number of other people have reported seeing the figure of a monk in the grounds attired in a *brown* habit with a white girdle about his waist, which is the garb worn by the Franciscans. If both these descriptions can be relied upon — and Mrs. Bodinar is quite certain that her monk was clothed in black — then we have not one but two ghost monks wandering around at Rosemorran, each representing a different monastic order!

*Lake's Parochial History of Cornwall, 1867.

The Roddas have encountered no ghosts inside the house, but they do have a strange problem with a door. It is a large, heavy oak door connencting the lounge with the drawing-room, and the problem is that it will not remain closed. The previous owners had the same trouble with it, and even called in a carpenter to look at it, but he could find nothing amiss. My wife and I examined the door minutely, then we closed it, noting that the latch engaged properly, and threw our combined weights against it. We are convinced that there is no way it could be opened other than by turning the handle.

Before Mr. Rodda acquired the property Rosemorran was owned and lived in by a Captain Malone, together with his wife and their daughter Ann. The original home of this distinguished family was nearby Trevaylor, but on the death of his father Captain Malone disposed of the estate and came to Rosemorran, shedding most of the large domestic staff but retaining the services of the housekeeper, Mrs. Clara Jenkins. I called on Mrs. Jenkins, now retired and living at Hayle, and asked her if she knew anything about this door and its eccentric behaviour.

She told me that whenever renovations were carried out at the house a palpable feeling of hostility invaded the whole place. 'It was a very weird sensation,' she said, 'as if the house resented being interfered with.' During a period when the drawing-room ceiling was being repaired they found it impossible to keep the door shut, even by jamming it with wads of paper, and it was on this occasion that they called in a carpenter. Mrs. Jenkins was interested but not surprised to learn that this nuisance still persists. She confided to me that there were times when, alone in the lounge or the drawing-room, she has watched the door slowly opening, but: 'I told no one in the house about it. That door used to give Miss Ann the creeps!'

She remembers, one Christmastide, entering the lounge to find the tree stripped of its decorations, which had been flung all around the floor, an example of supernatural vandalism which confirms her description of a resentful, and in this case downright vindictive influence which seems to have cast its shadow over the house from time to time.

But there were sweeter memories. 'Miss Ann came down to breakfast one morning and asked me if I had noticed a scent of honeysuckle. As a matter of fact I had often noticed it, yet no honeysuckle grew anywhere in the garden, and neither of us wore a perfume of any sort. You could smell this lovely scent even at times of the year when honeysuckle wasn't in bloom.'

Close to the house, at its eastern end, there is a little walled garden, partly hidden during the summer months by a thick growth of ferns, in the centre of which is a very old cherry tree. A few steps lead down to this quiet and peaceful place. But according to Mrs. Bodinar, a powerful supernatural force surrounds the area near the tree. 'I cannot work there,' she told me. 'It is as though a barrier is put up to stop me. Everything I try to do there takes hours rather than minutes, and once I was hit over the head and found myself lying at the foot of the steps.'

What are we to make of this diverse hotchpotch of psychic evidence? The two violent episodes of the Christmas tree and the walled garden do at least provide clues of a sort, tenuous but worth considering: A monastery is of course essentially a male preserve. The little garden may have been a monk's cemetery, or perhaps an altar, bearing in mind its location at the east end of the grounds, in which case the intrusion of Mrs. Bodinar, or any other woman for that matter, might well provoke a hostile reaction.

With regard to the decorated Christmas tree, its cheerful presence, something we take for granted as part of the Nativity celebrations, would doubtless be looked upon as frivolous if not pagan by these holy men, who would seek to destroy it. After all, Christmas trees in the home are a nineteenth-century innovation, at least in Britain, and would be quite incomprehensible to a mediaeval monk.

Chapter Thirteen

LIVING WITH GHOSTS

WHEN I called recently at a house in Lelant to follow up the story of a ghost dog seen pottering about the rooms and grounds, I gathered much more than I had bargained for in the way of strange tales.

The owners of this lovely house overlooking the Hayle estuary are South African-born Mr. Colin Silbert and his Canadian friend and business partner Mr. Dennis Hill, both of whose various encounters with the supernatural extend over a number of years, although neither of them will admit to possessing psychic powers.

Their first encounter with a ghost occured at a time when they were sharing an apartment in London. Tinkling sounds, which seemed to be coming from a chandelier above their heads began to puzzle them, since there was no draught in the room and no apparent movement from the chandelier itself. A clairvoyant friend, visiting their flat for the first time, began to look closely round the sitting-room, and on being asked if she was searching for something replied: 'Yes, a bell. I can't see it. Was there one, low on a shelf?' Mr. Silbert told her that there had indeed been a bell near where they were sitting, on a coffee table, but: 'we moved it to a higher shelf.'

'Then will you please put it back,' the medium said, 'there is a little girl who comes here. She says she can't reach it up there, and she likes to play with it.'

Mr. Silbert then revealed that a five-year-old niece of his had died in South Africa, but whether they were able to establish that this was the true identity of the little ghost I do not know. I hope, however, that they remembered to put the bell back on the coffee table!

Later, the two friends moved to a house in Fulham, and soon found that they were sharing it with the ghost of a monk. 'We saw him often, and quite plainly,' Mr. Hill told me. 'And so did other people staying with us. We think he was of the Franciscan order, for the brown cloak and hood could be seen clearly. He would wander about the house, and once I saw him go up the stairs.'

He seems to have been a benign and friendly figure, for his presence brought only sensations of peace and harmony, never of fear. Even Mr. Hill's cat and dog showed no signs of alarm although obviously aware of the ghost.

The Borough of Fulham contains, of course, the famous palace, manor-house of successive bishops of London, part of which dates from the time of Henry the Seventh, and it is likely that the house occupied by Mr. Silbert and Mr. Hill was built on the site of a religious place of some sort. There seems no other explanation for the presence of a ghostly monk in a twentieth-century house.

But the next event was more disturbing. Mr. Silbert at about this time was proprietor of an antique shop in the London area, and upon entering his premises one morning he saw that a large Victorian painting, which should have been hanging on the wall, had slipped to the floor. After noting that it had suffered no damage Mr. Silbert hammered another nail into the wall and re-hung the painting. The following morning it was again on the floor, and this time one of the two hooks to which the cord was attached had come away from the back of the frame. The exasperated proprietor screwed it back and the next morning was relieved to find the painting in its place on the wall. But worse was to follow.

'I had been out buying,' Mr. Silbert said, 'and among the items I had picked up were two elegant opaline vases which I had hoped to sell to some American dealers. I placed all the items on a marble topped table and walked downstairs to another part of my shop, when suddenly there was a most awful crash. I rushed upstairs thinking someone had come through the window, instead of which I found that a chandelier had fallen from the ceiling on to the marble table. Nothing showed any sign of damage, neither the chandelier, the table, nor most of the things I had placed there except the two vases, which were smashed to smithereens.'

Mr. Silbert and his friend came to the conclusion that it was time to call in their clairvoyant friend, but the lady was indisposed and sent in her place a young medium by the name of Ann, somewhat inexperienced and unknown to the two men. After some preamble Ann asked if the name 'Katie' had any significance for them. The startled Mr. Silbert admitted that he had a particular friend of that name who had died in a fire three weeks previously, or was presumed to have done so, but according to the medium 'Katie' had not died in the fire and had been desperately trying to attract his attention in order to give him the true facts surrounding her death. The medium concluded by assuring him that the demonstrations at the shop were at an end. 'In future,' she told him, whenever your friend Katie is around the lights will flicker. Just say 'O.K. Katie, we know you are there,' and the flickering will stop.'

Mr. Silbert told me that this in fact did happen, and still does in their Cornish home, but since lights occasionally flicker in most houses for reasons which have no connection with the presence of spirits, one feels that 'Katie' would have done better to select a less ambiguous way of announcing herself.

66

'Then we came to Cornwall on holiday,' Mr. Hill recalled, and we went to a shop in Hayle and bought an old painting of St. Michael's Mount, not to re-sell but to keep for ourselves, and took it back to our London flat, where it remained for two or three years. Eventually we bought a little holiday cottage in St. John's-street, Hayle, which we had to have pretty well gutted and rebuilt, with a room or two added. The first night we settled in, I woke up at three o'clock in the morning and there was this old lady standing at the foot of the bed, smiling happily at me. When later I described her to some local people they told me I must have seen the ghost of Lucy Jenkins, who used to own the cottage.'

Some time after this they made a remarkable discovery. The painting of St. Michael's Mount, which had languished in their London flat but now hung in the cottage, had belonged to Lucy Jenkins. It appears that the second-hand dealers from whom they bought it had been called in to clear the cottage after her death. Perhaps this was what made the old lady happy — her painting had come home!

When the two friends finally decided to retire from business they decided to settle in Cornwall, and acquired the house in Lelant. But they are still not free from the supernatural. The ghost of a dog, which they describe as looking like a young Labrador retriever, roams around the house. 'Sometimes he is absent for long periods,' Mr. Hill told me, 'then we see him quite a bit.' The dog's presence is a mystery, because the house is little more than fifty years old, and a dog belonging to the previous owners left with them, alive and well.

But if we do not know who this lone prowler is, we wish him well, and if for whatever reason he is going to continue his visits to what is presumably his old home, he will I am sure always receive a kindly welcome from the two gentlemen who live there now. They know quite a lot about ghosts!

Chapter Fourteen

BRIEF ENCOUNTERS

I SUSPECT that most people will have experienced at least one supernatural incident in their lives, probably without attaching much importance to it, or even remembering it with the passing of the years.

I have talked to scores of people who were willing to tell me of strange and inexplicable things which had happened to them or to their friends and relatives, yet sadly many of these events are too perfunctory in the telling or too lacking in narrative content to warrant inclusion in these pages. As a kind of postscript however, I have selected a few such items from around this area which I feel are deserving of mention, and which perhaps make up in uniqueness where they fail in the matter of graphic detail.

West of Lelant Downs stands the splendid Trencrom Hill, presented to the National Trust in 1946 by Colonel H. G. Tyringham as a memorial to the men and women of Cornwall who gave their lives in the two world wars. At the summit it is 550 feet above sea level and commands a staggering view of both the North and South coasts. Archaeologists tell us that it was almost certainly occupied by the early Iron Age people and again much later by the Cornish during the so-called Dark Ages, between the end of Roman rule and the Norman conquest.

In recent years (or perhaps not so recent — I can quote only from contemporary sources) the area around Trencrom has been associated with strange happenings which have led some local people to believe that the hill is haunted by the spirits of those primitive tribes, and I have to say that the nature of some of these incidents does suggest something of the sort.

One August morning in 1964, Mr. Reg Barton from Northampton, accompanied by his wife and two friends, was driving his car along the narrow road which leads from Lelant Downs to the village of Cripple's Ease. They had reached the point where this road briefly skirts the edge of Trencrom Hill when the car engine spluttered and died. Mr. Barton knew that the petrol tank was nearly full, so he climbed out of the car and lifted the bonnet in the hope of locating the trouble, but there was no shortage of oil or water, nor had the engine apparently overheated. He returned to the car and was about to try the starter when he became aware of the figure of a man 'wearing peculiar clothes' staring at him from the roadway. All the other occupants of the car saw the figure briefly before it vanished. Mr. Barton turned the starter key, and to his relief the engine sprang to life, enabling the scared quartet to beat a hasty exit.

Pedestrians and motorists alike travelling this stretch of road after dark have spoken of seeing blue points of light moving towards them, and visitors who have climbed to the summit of the hill itself — not a difficult task, for the ascent is gradual — describe an eerie feeling as though being watched by unseen eyes.

(I was not surprised to learn this. Some years ago, walking my dog across neighbouring Rosewall Hill, I noticed that he showed totally uncharacteristic signs of fear, repeatedly stopping in his tracks and looking around him with raised hackles. At the time I assumed that he had picked up the scent of wild goats which have been roaming these hills for years, but in the light of the above information I have since considered other possible reasons!).

Some of these stories may well have a rational explanation. Was the figure observed by the tourists a tramp or 'hippy' type, glimpsed briefly before he hid himself? Are the blue lights reflections from quartz crystals embedded in a wayside rock and caught in the headlights of approaching cars? Are the climbers to the summit influenced by pre-knowledge of Trencrom's supernatural reputation?

Perhaps, but one person who has no doubts as to the reality of her own ghostly experience at Trencrom is Miss Georgina Balcombe, a social worker now living in retirement.

'I had a severely disabled friend,' she told me, 'who lived with her mother in a cottage at the foot of Trencrom Hill. When the mother became ill and was taken away I went to see what I could do to clear up the cottage, which had become very neglected and in need of repair. Another friend, Paula Blake, came with me and together we set about plastering up the walls and doing whatever immediate jobs were necessary to make the place habitable. Then, one day, I was clearing out an old cupboard on my own in an upstairs room when there was a terrific crash from below. I went down to investigate and found all the tools we had been working with scattered all over the floor.'

From that point the bangings and throwing around of articles continued unabated, but the two women valiantly carried on with their work until they finally became so accustomed to the Poltergeist tantrums that, whilst they could not entirely ignore it, they did tell it to 'shut up' from time to time, and to leave them in peace, with what success I do not know.

My wife and I heard this story when we visited Miss Balcombe at her sixteenth-century cottage, the garden of which overlooks a beautiful stretch of the Restronguet Creek near Devoran. She told us how, on an impulse, she gave up her job as Assistant Surgical Nurse to a veterinary establishment in Esher and enrolled for a course of training in the care of mentally handicapped children. Later, she came to Cornwall and became, I understand, the first teacher in the County to undertake this work in a full-time capacity. In 1953 she bought the cottage through an agency without even bothering to go and look at it first, and in the event it proved to be a happy decision. She soon found, however, that she was sharing her home with the ghost of a previous owner, a well-known character called Annie Marshall, who had spent much of her life caring for sick and unwanted animals including, up to the time she was taken away to die in an old peoples' home, no less than thirty cats. Annie's ghost has been seen, but not by Miss Balcombe, who nevertheless senses her presence so strongly that she feels impelled to talk aloud to her.

Although it is many years since she retired, Miss Balcombe still makes herself available whenever a child or an animal is in need of her services. 'Whenever I feel Annie's presence near me,' she told us, 'I know that within a short time somebody is going to call or 'phone me about a sick animal or a child who needs my help. It as if she arranges it.'

Despite advancing years — she was approaching her eightieth birthday at the time of our meeting — Miss Balcombe is a lady possessing immense vitality and a zest for adventurous living. A dedicated traveller with a penchant for cold climes, she has traversed a sizeable area of the Canadian North-West territories and penetrated into the Arctic Circle, where she befriended Eskimo families and slept in an igloo. Such a lady does not strike one as being given to flights of fancy, and if Miss Balcombe tells me that she is in telepathic communication with the ghost of Annie Marshall, I for one am ready to believe her.

The Wayside Museum at Zennor, with its remarkable collection of Tin-mining tools, early farming implements and domestic appliances, presents a striking visual account of eighteenth and nineteenth-century life in this once isolated area of Cornwall. The museum was at one time a mill, and the building housing original machinery and millstones still stands, as does the old blacksmith's shop, complete with forge and an array of iron objects specially made for the use of villagers in their homes and farmsteads. The adjacent 'Miller's House,' a delightful cottage which is certainly over two hundred years old, contains a kitchen with an open hearth and steel-lined baking oven, together with a unique assemblage of early Cornish cooking utensils. The museum curators, Mr. and Mrs. R. G. Williamson, told me that this cottage was the scene of an extraordinary incident a few years ago.

A Welshman and his wife had drifted in to take a look at the kitchen, but the moment they entered the cottage the man burst into tears and staggered out, insisting that the place was evil and 'full of sadness and misery.' He could not be induced to go back in, but curiously enough the same couple turned up again the following year. This time the woman entered the cottage but her husband would not go near it.

Ancient buildings, saturated in human history, do of course affect sensitive people to some degree, but this does seem a rather extreme case! The Williamsons tell me they are unaware of any supernatural presence in the cottage.

During the period when the Bochym stories were receiving our attention (Chapter 10) my wife and I chanced to visit the Old Inn down at Mullion. Sadly, there is a shortage of historical data about this marvellously evocative and very ancient tavern, so that I am indebted to Arthur Caddick's delightful 'Illustrated Guide to One Hundred Inns' for telling me that its history goes back to the fifteenth-century and that in more recent times Marconi was a frequent visitor. In fact, Poldhu, from where the first ever radio message was transmitted, is only a mile or so down the road.

I asked the landlord, Mr. Jack Gayton, if the Old Inn had a ghost. For an answer he took us through to the guest wing and introduced us to an employee, Mrs. Vera George, busy with her Hoover in one of the bedrooms.

She pointed to the bed. 'Sometimes when I am making it,' she told us, 'I suddenly feel a presence in the room. Then my neck is grabbed from behind and I am pulled upwards and away from the bed. My body feels icy cold for a time, but I don't feel especially frightened. The ghost seems quite friendly.'

It did not sound like a very friendly gesture to me, unless the ghost was pulling her away from what had perhaps in the past been a dangerous spot. I asked what was beneath the room in which we were standing, and it seems the guest rooms are an extension, built over an ancient storage cellar. Perhaps there was a trap-door or a loft above the cellar. We can only guess. The Inn was at one time owned by a certain Mary Mundy, who seems to be something of a local legend, and Mrs. George thinks that Mary may be the ghost.

I asked her why she should think the ghost is a woman, and her reply was as unexpected as it was memorable. 'If it is a man,' she said, 'he would probably shove me down on the bed, not pull me away from it.'